W9-BSZ-080

Overcoming ADHD WIthout Medication

A Parent and Educator's Guidebook

Overcoming ADHD WIthout Medication
A Parent and Educator's Guidebook

Attention Deficit Hyperactivity Disorder (ADHD)
is a battle that can be won
without the need for medication

The Association for Youth, Children
and Natural Psychology

Newark Psychological and Educational Publications
Newark, NJ

College of the Ouachitas

Overcoming
ADHD without Medication
A Guidebook for Parents and Teachers
English

Printed in the USA
Newark Psychological and Educational Publications
Newark, NJ

ISBN-10: 1449902871
ISBN-13: 9781449902872

Copyright © 2011 AYCNP
All rights reserved. This book may not be reproduced for commercial purposes. Quotes of more than 100 words, only with written permission, including online resources.

Library of Congress Control No. 2010936531

Photos on cover or elsewhere in this book, or quotes from authorities in the opening pages of this book or throughout the book, do not necessarily signify an endorsement of the views expressed here, or of this book, unless otherwise stated.

Cover Photo: 1. istockphoto.com Miroslav Ferkuniak 2. istockphoto.com kzenon 3. istockphoto.com Abejon Photography 4. istockphoto.com Amie Pastoor 5. Shutterstock AFH 6. Aaron Escobar 7. U.S. Census Bureau 8. Shutterstock.com absolute-india 9. Unique Art 10. Shutterstock.com Olga Sapegina.

RJ
506
.H9
O75
2011

This book is dedicated to the children of Paterson, Newark and Jersey City, NJ

Acknowledgements

Special thanks to Joel Nigg from Michigan State University for his inspiring work and help. Thanks to Carol Confehr, for her support and insight from her work with children. Thanks also to Jackie McGraw from Paterson, NJ Public Library and her work with children, and who inspired the research that went into this book. Also, thanks to Russell Barkley who gave help and guidance. Thanks also to J.W. for his kind help with editing and to M.W. for her support. Also to Keisha Hill for her support and insight, as well as Kim Booker, in Paterson, NJ for her passionate dedication to help her students.

Important Note – Please Read

The information presented in this book is intended for informative and educational purposes and not as a medical directive. This book was produced by educators rather than psychologists, although much of the information in this book was derived from the work of psychologists and other professionals. By reading this publication the reader acknowledges that he or she maintains full responsibility in treatment choices for him or herself or for one's children or for children under one's care.

This book does not replace professional treatment if necessary, but rather, complements it. By reading this book, the reader acknowledges his or her own freedom of choice in seeking medical treatment, and agrees that the Association for Youth, Children and Natural Psychology, as well as any individuals associated with the Association for Youth, Children and Natural Psychology, including authors quoted in this book, bear no responsibility for one's own personal choices in mental health or other medical treatment for him or herself or for one's children.

Readers are encouraged to gather as much information as possible from a variety of reliable sources when making medical choices involving mental health, evaluate the options, and make informed and balanced decisions.

Anyone who him or herself experiences suicidal thoughts, or anyone whose children are experiencing suicidal thoughts, should seek support from qualified professionals.

Preface

My first encounter with the topic of attention deficit disorder (ADD) and attention deficit hyperactivity disorder (ADHD) was in a book written by Sandra Reif, in the Spring of 2005 in a grade school in Paterson, NJ, How to Reach and Teach ADD/ADHD Children, a book written in 1987 that is still widely read by teachers. In the school where I encountered Sandra Reif's book, there was a student with wide open, slightly panicky eyes who stated that he played five hours of video games a day. He exclaimed that he knew he played too many hours of video games, wanted to stop, "but can't".

In the same school students would watch non-educational fast-paced movies on down-time that seemed to wind them up. However, when these same grade school students were given the option of watching movies and learning drawing techniques, about 80% opted for the art and became engrossed in it.

One student about nine years old confided in me that he was on medication because of his behavior problems. He had a hard time sitting in class and was a bit of a problem to his teachers and parents. He didn't like the medication, stating that, they say that the medication is "giving me control, but they are controlling me." He felt cornered and frustrated. The same student stated that he watched three hours of television per day, including the Comedy Channel (not for children), in addition to video games.

One young child who was in the process of being classified, most likely with ADHD, came from an unstructured family where it is probable that he received very little attention or was neglected. He could not accomplish any of his classwork and the teacher who had close to 30 students, couldn't handle him. However, after one week with a personal assistant, he was able to keep up with the schoolwork on the same level as the other children, and his whole attitude changed.

Another nine-year-old boy from another major school district in New Jersey, was a full one year behind in his math skills. He was in the fourth grade, but could only perform at an early third grade level. He could not concentrate on his schoolwork in school or at home and was distracted. If the problem had persisted, he would have most likely been classified with a form of ADHD, which in most cases involves prescription treatment. His father hired a tutor and also made some changes at home. The children could no longer watch television, movies or video games during the week, which they had been doing as a matter of habit, directly after school for at least an hour or more daily. They could watch television, movies and play video games only on the weekends.

After approximately three months of tutoring, and after one or two months with new limits at home, the boy was able to concentrate, and went from D's to B's and A's in math within six months, making the honor role for the first time. He was able to concentrate on his schoolwork and math, as well as perform at a level appropriate for his grade. Prevention is important for all parents to consider and Overcoming ADHD Without Medication is an attainable goal for the vast majority of children and teens.

Contents

Chapter 5
Educational Solutions

Chapter 6
Resources

65

Introduction

"Masking the symptoms rather than removing the cause of the problems has always retarded the development of community health. The most fruitful area of research would be in prevention." Lawrence Green, Ph.D., J.M Ottoson, Ph.D., 1999. Community Population and Health

A reading coaching from the Paterson, NJ public library spoke for a long time about her experience with children who had ADHD. She felt that the vast majority of them could be helped if their parents were given support and educated in how to help their children, through positive changes in their diet, and with support from services such as provided by the library program in terms of individual attention after school. She felt that in all her years of professional work, having helped hundreds of children who had been classified as ADHD, or who had serious symptoms of ADHD, she had only encountered three who she felt were truly ADHD. In those cases, none of these three students had gone on medication, and were helped without medication through non-pharmaceutical professional support and simple lifestyle changes that parents were encouraged to implement.

Through working with scores if not a hundred or more students with ADHD or on the border of being classified, and through much research, interviews, phone interviews and email interchanges with professionals and organizations in the field, and through interchanges with teachers, special education teachers, psychologists and school psychologists, social workers, nurses and school principals, as well as the afore-mentioned reading coach, this book was produced.

The basis for the book commenced in 2005 and 2006, and reflects the lifework of many dedicated professionals. It endeavors to present the information in a simple and concise form that is easily assimilated by busy parents and teachers, so that children might have a fuller opportunity for a ADHD symptom-free childhood through their teenage years.

Supplementary material from Illinois State professor Daniella Barroqueira, Ph.D., who herself has ADHD, and whose experience is mirrored by a Newark grade school art teacher referred to in the same location of the book, helps to support the view that art can help some children, youth and adults, to cope with and overcome symptoms of ADHD, that some children and youth with ADHD are highly visual and creative, and that the negative of ADHD, can be turned into a positive.

A grade school art teacher and colleague who had been labeled ADHD and took Ritalin, and later, Adderall, through middle school and high school, explained that what he disliked the most about it was "the label". It made him different, set apart, from the other kids. When he was on the stimulants, he never felt himself, and the medicine contributed to anger problems. He said that what did help, was when he went to college, immersing himself in art and playing soccer. The art helped him to focus and the soccer was just the right therapy for his hyperactivity. Now, as a teacher, he is well adjusted and helps children, many

1

of whom, have some of the same symptoms he dealt with when he was in school.

David Rabiner, Ph.D. of Duke University provides material on medication for ADHD, presenting both sides of the issue (whereas this book endeavors to encourage non-pharmaceutical interventions), as well as providing supplementary information on childhood depression, was is often co-morbid with symptoms of ADHD.

Additionally, an Iowa State University study is included in the supplementary material section, which provides scientific support for the view that violent video games can affect a child's level of aggression, as well as contribute to symptoms of ADHD, something that has been observed by many, but that has been lacking in actual proof.

Joel Nigg, Ph.D., of Michigan State University, who graciously helped in the early stages of putting together the material that led to this book, and who authored the book, What Causes ADHD?, suggested in his book that playing violent video games might be contributing factor to symptoms of ADHD and the actual disorder. (Professor Nigg provides support for the idea that there are a wide range of factors, including environmental, that might contribute to ADHD, providing scientific evidence, as well as suggesting that a number of factors need to be further researched). Since the time of Dr. Nigg's research, there seems to be more direct evidence for the link between video game play and ADHD. Russell Barkley, Ph.D., whose work is referred to in this book, also kindly provided guidance and offered opinions which led to the formulation of some of the material here.

There are many others whose work has been used in connection with this book, and it is hoped that this information can help parents specifically, to help their children overcome symptoms of ADHD without medication. Even if a parent chooses to have his child take medication for ADHD, the principles in this book can be of value, and can help the child to experience symptoms to a lesser degree. There is no book that provides all the answers to any medical, psychological or behavioral problem. However, educating oneself with various viewpoints and perspectives is the course of wisdom, and can contribute to a greater chance for success.

Chapter 1

What is ADHD?

We've gotten used to taking pills for much that ails us. But prescription drugs are not infallible and many have been pulled from the market or slapped with a warning by the FDA, due to health-threatening side effects. We don't lack for alternatives. Plenty of research shows that exercise, diet, and other lifestyle changes are effective weapons...

Let's be honest: there's a wonderful convenience to taking a pill. It's just so much easier than changing what we eat, mustering up the time and willpower to exercise...

From: *Beyond pills: 5 conditions you can improve with lifestyle changes.*
Harvard Health Newsletter

What is ADHD?

Jennifer's son Matt had always been difficult. He would tear through the house like a tornado, shouting, kicking and jumping off furniture. Nothing kept his interest for longer than a few minutes, and he would often run off without warning and mid-sentence, unconcerned about bumping into anyone or anything.

Jennifer was exhausted, but when Matt was in preschool, she wasn't too concerned because she guessed, "boys will be boys."

However, it was a struggle to try to get Matt to cooperate, and when he entered third grade, his disruptive behavior and inattention in class raised the red flag of his teacher. Jennifer took Matt to the pediatrician, who, after a short interview, informed Jennifer that Matt most likely had ADHD. The best thing would be to prescribe stimulant medications, which he might not need to take for the rest of his life, but most likely for the rest of his school years.

Jennifer was relieved and concerned at the same time. While she was happy to hear that Matt had a diagnosable condition, the prospect of her son being on medication for five or more years distressed her. Was medication really necessary? Is ADHD really a condition, were some of her questions. What about the side effects? What would the medication do to his body? The pediatrician reassured Jennifer that everything would work out fine, and sent her home with a prescription.

Some Symptoms of ADHD:

There are many symptoms associated with ADHD, including the following:

- *Poor concentration, distractibility, impulsive behavior, careless mistakes, difficulty in controlling anger.*
- *Inability to complete tasks, difficulty sustaining attention towards tasks.*
- *Hyperactive behavior, excessive activity, fidgeting, squirming, running, climbing excessively.*
- *Poor listening skills.*
- *Talking excessively, blurting out answers before hearing the whole question.*

David Rabiner, from Duke University, an expert on ADHD, describes Attention Deficit Hyperactivity Disorder (ADHD), as *"a disorder characterized by a persistent pattern of inattention and/or hyperactivity/impulsivity that occurs in academic, occupational, or social settings."*

Some of the problems associated with ADHD include, making careless mistakes, failure to complete tasks, difficulty staying organized and becoming easily distracted.

Some other issues are associated with hyperactivity, such as fidgetiness and squirminess, running excessively or climbing, inability to exercise self-control or sit still in class, inappropriate or excessive talking, being constantly on the go, impulsivity and impatience, difficulty waiting one's turn, blurting out answers in class and frequent interrupting, among other problems.

Rabiner explains that "Although many individuals with ADHD display both inattentive and hyperactive/impulsive symptoms, some individuals show symptoms from one group but not the other."

Who is affected by symptoms of ADHD?

- ADHD is usually considered to be a childhood condition but its symptoms can be present with some adults as well.
- ADHD symptoms are manifest with poor concentration, impulse control, lack of attention or focus. ADHD sometimes includes hyperactivity, which may be the case in perhaps 40-70% of ADHD diagnoses.
- 3-10% of children in each state (U.S.) - 2.5 million school age children - are diagnosed with ADHD.
- Up to 2/3 of children who are diagnosed with ADHD also have a secondary disorder such as depression, an anxiety disorder or Tourette Syndrome, or they may also be diagnosed with Oppositional Defiant Disorder (ODD) or Conduct Disorder (CD) [1]

---

[1]   Ashley, S., Ph.D., 2005.

Since every child displays some of the symptoms associated with ADHD, when is ADHD diagnosed? Simply put, when symptoms are prolonged and disruptive to the daily life of the child (or adult).

ADHD and School

ADHD most frequently is initially addressed through the school system. A teacher may often raise the first red flag. The child is evaluated and a child study team works with the child, teachers and parents. If a certain number of symptoms are considered to reach a level of intensity and duration to the point that it interferes with a child's ability to sustain day to day activities over an extended period of time, this can result in label of ADHD for the child.

The benefit of this is that it enables educators and the child study team to give extra time and attention to the individual child. A personal assistant might be made available also. Parents can take appropriate measure to educate themselves and make adjustments in their parenting and this might help to offset the child's predisposition towards hyperactivity or distractibility. Educators can also work at providing positive educational solutions for these individual students. The extra attention given to a child in many forms, along with adjustments that parents might make, often can be key factors in a child's improvement.

When educators and psychologists make a diagnosis of disorders such as ADHD, there is usually a certain amount of subjectivity in the interpretation of the symptoms, that is, it depends on how an individual psychologist or team views and interprets these symptoms. Computer aided tests are also interpreted subjectively rather than being purely scientific.

It is generally recognized that stimulant medications do not usually, or necessarily, significantly increase grade performance. Parents should not expect significant improvement in grades due to administering of stimulant medication. (Eide & Eide, 2006).*

---

* Those studies which attribute increased grade performance to medication, usually do not delineate between the benefits of the medication, and that of any of a number of other interventions being administered at the same time, giving a misleading impression that the positive academic gains are attributable to medicaton, when in fact, they may be the result of therapy, special education, increased attention being given to the child, or other changes.

Labeling of Psychiatric Disorders

To be noted: Not all agree with the labeling system as it relates to many psychiatric disorders.[2] A tendency has developed based on what is known as the "medical model" of psychiatry, which is the most common platform in 21st century psychiatry, but not necessarily universally accepted, even in the professional community.[3] Additionally, there are other models of psychology which help to more fully explain the various dynamics involved in the development of mental health disorders and for mental health in general.[4]

The medical model involves identifying symptoms, matching symptoms to a list that has been denoted in the DSM-IV, the psychiatric book of disorders, determining a label for the disorder, and prescribing what is deemed appropriate medication for that label. Therapy is sometimes used in conjunction with drug treatment. However, in modern psychiatry, based on the "medical model", therapy, educational remediation, parental training, or psycho-education, is often given secondary consideration, and sometimes given very little, if any, consideration. In reality, self help and lifestyle changes need to be considered with any psychiatric diagnosis, and in giving attention to these, many, or even most of the symptoms of ADHD can be addressed.

The American Psychiatric Association's Diagnostic and Statistical Manual-IV, Text Revision DSM-IV-TR, is used by mental health professionals to diagnose mental health disorders. ADHD refers to attention deficit hyperactivity disorder, and what has been commonly referred to in the past as ADD, or attention deficit disorder. The DSM-IV-TR breaks down ADHD into three sub-classifications: ADHD , *Combined Type;* which includes symptoms typical of ADHD, along with hyperactivity and impulsivity; ADHD, Predominantly Inattentive Type, what has been referred to in the past as ADD, or attention deficit disorder, without significant hyperactivity or impulsivity; ADHD, *Predominantly Hyperactive-Impulsive Type,* when distractibility and inattentiveness is not significant. See: *Center for Disease Control and Prevention (CDC),* Attention-Deficit / Hyperactivity Disorder (ADHD) - Symptoms and Diagnosis.

---

[2]   Eide, B., et al., 2006.

[3]   Olfman, 2007.

[4]   Urie Bronfenbrenner, 2008. New World Encyclopedia.

Studies have indicated that children who spend time outdoors can receive benefits of a positive reduction in symptoms of ADHD as a direct result. (Kuo, F.E., Ph.D., Taylor, A., Ph.D., 2004). It is also possible that children who watch less television (or who spend less time playing video games), might also benefit in terms of a reduction in the intensity of symptoms associated with ADHD. (Cristakis, D., 2004)

Some parents who have cut out TV and video games for their children during the week, have seen a dramatic improvement in the ability of their children to concentrate on their schoolwork and to focus.[5] Some have found that attention to diet results in positive benefits in one's symptom profile. (Personal notes, observations from J. McNuff, 2005).

The labeling of the symptoms of ADHD as considered in this book, is a practice that can be controversial, and that in some countries (such as Britain), has been resisted by the professional community up until fairly recently. (Britain has not been so readily disposed to prescribe medication for ADHD as has the U.S.) Additionally, the practice of labeling a person, "my son *is* ADHD," "my daughter *is* bipolar," is also something that is not encouraged by many, including many advocacy groups and government mental health agencies. Therefore, this book tries to avoid labeling those who have symptoms of ADHD as *being* ADHD, but rather as having symptoms which are associated with ADHD.

An excellent and balanced resource on the issue of labeling in mental health, especially as it relates to children and teens, is the book, *Please Don't Label My Child,* by Scott Shannon, Ph.D., a child psychiatrist with years of experience in helping children, and parents with a wide variety of psychiatric issues.

---

[5] New Jersey Teaching Notes, 2008.

Single Parent Families

A disproportional number of children from single parent homes are diagnosed with ADHD. Poor family structure can be a factor.[6]   Lack of control in home can lead to problems in the school. However, other factors can be involved. Children need love, time and attention from parents and strong emotional attachments. When these are lacking, it can contribute to behavioral and attentional problems in school.

Many sincere single parents struggle to make a living and to provide a loving home in which to raise a child. The challenges of both working and raising a family can leave one with little energy at the end of the day, and it can be challenging to meet both the physical and emotional demands of raising children. This can make it difficult for some parents to provide the ideal situation for their children. [7]

Photo: www.istockphoto.com   Miroslav Ferkuniak

---

[6] Bee, H., et al., 2007.

[7] Hill, K., 2006.

Many principals and teachers are a source of unconditional love for children, who might not otherwise receive acceptance or love in their lives. Because teaching style can make a significant difference in the life and success of a child, teachers are encouraged to be patient and to help children to succeed, as well as avoid being unreasonable or harsh. Children are often in school for the better part of the day, many are in after-school programs, including those which help children with homework.

Much is expected of teachers in terms of helping children to perform well academically, but it must also be noted that there are factors in school, at home, and in the community, which can contribute to a child's difficulties in succeeding academically. There are multi-faceted dynamics involved in a child's success, and this is most likely true with mental health issues such as ADHD as well. (See Urie Bronfenbrenner's bioecological model of mental health, in contrast to the "medical model" of mental health, which is commonly used as a foundation for labeling and drug treatment).

What Causes ADHD?

Joel Nigg, Ph.D., author of the scientifically-oriented book, What Causes ADHD?, who is an associate professor of psychology at Michigan State University, conveys the idea that the causes for ADHD can be many and varied, but that there *are* causes. Some of these can be:

Prenatal

- Prenatal exposure to drugs, alcohol and smoking.
- Prenatal exposure to some prescription drugs.
- Babies born prematurely have a greater risk of symptoms associated with ADHD.

Causes of ADHD, continued

Genetic factors - Children may be born with a predisposition towards the symptoms of ADHD or depression. Other children in the same household, who are not genetically predisposed, might not develop these same symptoms.

Environmental factors - There is some evidence that certain environmental contaminants[8] can contribute to the development of symptoms of ADHD in certain children. Some that are mentioned by name are PCB's, lead and mercury overexposure or poisoning. (Nigg, J., 2005).

Social factors

At home - The need for strong emotional attachments, or lack thereof, can contribute to symptoms of ADHD. Family problems, family instability, or a disorderly home can be contributing factors in a child's inability to concentrate or focus for some children.

At school - There is some evidence that the classroom environment might be one area where attention can be given with regard to improving some symptoms associated with ADHD.
(Rabiner, March 2010. Also, Focusing on Instruction, *Teach ADHD*).

Social factors - Social isolation or the need for friendships and positive (non-electronic) recreation might also be contributing factors in some of the symptoms associated with ADHD.

---

[8] Nigg, J., 2006.

Physical Needs

The need for good diet and nutrition, exercise, can be of importance when considering both childhood and adult ADHD. This can also be true for depression. Diets low in sugar and low in refined carbohydrates can help for good general health, but can also contribute to good mental health.

This can mean doing without donuts, cakes, candies, cookies, white flour, white rice - instead, eat whole grain foods, brown rice, whole wheat flour and healthy snacks, as a general rule of thumb, and without taking it to extremes. This can be of some help for many children with ADHD symptoms. Providing snacks which are natural, rather than highly-processed foods which may have many added chemicals and additives, can make a positive difference. Mayo Clinic states that while it is unlikely that food additives cause ADHD, it is possible that hyperactivity might be aggravated by some food additives.

Children need to eat three healthful meals a day. A healthy, regular breakfast is essential for a child's ability to concentrate in school. If a child skips breakfast regularly or regularly eats high-sugar foods, it can contribute to some of the symptoms of ADHD and/or depression for children who have that predisposition, especially when present with other contributing factors. Girls who are diagnosed with ADHD, are more likely to be of the inattentive type, boys tend to be hyperactive (Mayo Clinic). It stands to reason, that for a girl who does not eat regularly, does not eat breakfast and skips other meals, this might be contributing to her symptoms of inattention. This has been observed in the classroom.

In Newark, NJ, implementation of a School Breakfast program resulted in a 95.7% participation during the 2008-9 school year. School breakfasts went from 8000 a day in 2004 to 25,000 per day during 2008-9. Other cities of note were Columbus, OH, and Boston, MA. (Essex News, February, 2010).

One of the problems, though, with school breakfasts, are that many are of very low nutritional value and high in sugar content: Fruit Loops, Apple Jacks, sugary muffins, Pop-Tarts, etc. There needs to be effort in many school districts to provide a consistently more-nutritious breakfast to children, one that is consistent with the health education that children and teens receive in class. Some school districts have done that.

Media - Long hours with the media, television, movies, video games, and Internet might affect the mind and behavior of many children. Content, such as violent content,[9] excessive action-violence or cartoon violence, as well as horror movies, and pornography[10] or sexually disorienting material, might also be factors which contribute to symptoms of ADHD, depression, or bipolar disorder, for some children, teens (or adults).

ADHD, bipolar disorder, and other disorders or conditions with similar symptoms

Symptoms that are evident with an ADHD diagnosis can also manifest themselves in disorders such as bipolar disorder. One clinical psychologist in a public school candidly acknowledged that "it is difficult to accurately diagnose disorders [such as ADHD and bipolar disorder] in children because the symptoms of the varying disorders overlap. The same symptoms often manifest themselves in different disorders." Psychiatrists might treat a client for both ADHD and bipolar disorder, or might mistakenly prescribe certain medications through an inaccurate diagnosis.

One of the reasons for this is that evaluations are most often subjective rather than being scientific. In one recent study, it was concluded that over half of the clients being treated for bipolar disorder were misdiagnosed. (Zimmerman,

---

[9] Nigg, J., 2006.

[10] Parents, stepparents, guardians, and anyone who works with children should realize that exposing under-age children to pornography or other non-educational sexual material may be considered a form of child abuse or gross neglect in some states. Many states have mandatory reporting laws for any form of suspected child abuse.

M., June, 2008, July, 2009). This was determined through a more-accurate, scientifically-oriented analysis of the symptoms of each respondent, than is usually the case. What was apparently true, in this study, of bipolar disorder of over- or misdiagnosis, may also be true of ADHD as well, suggests Sharna Olfman's research in *No Child Left Different*. Olfman is a clinical psychologist and associate professor of psychology at Point Park University in Pennsylvania.

Mayo Clinic states that there are symptoms that resemble ADHD in the following disorders or conditions: learning or language problems, mood disorders (such as anxiety or depression), hyperthyroidism, seizure disorders, fetal alcohol syndrome, vision or hearing problems, Tourette Syndrome, sleep disorders and autism. Also of note, some of these disorders are diagnosed in as many as one in three children diagnosed with ADHD.

ADHD is not life threatening

ADHD poses no imminent danger to a child. A child might be more accident prone, but with a little extra attention by parents, this needn't be a major concern and the probability of medicine fixing that problem is not certain. Of encouragement to parents is what is stated by Russell Barkley that ADHD is not "a pathological condition or a disease stage". Rather, it is a "natural or developmental form" of the disorder ADHD, and then, "should not be considered some grossly abnormal pathological condition." Instead, it is described as a condition that is "not qualitatively or categorically different from normal at all, but likely to be the extreme lower end of a normal trait. Thus the difference is really just a matter of degree and not a truly qualitative difference from normal." Dr. Barkley states, "this should help everyone view ADHD from a kinder perspective."[11]

---

[11] Barkley, 1997.

14

Mistaken Identity: *Child Abuse and Sleep Disorders are often misdiagnosed as ADHD*

Child Abuse - Children who have been sexually abused have mistakenly been treated for ADHD or bipolar disorder. Treatment and care for children who may have been victims of child abuse of any type is much different than the treatment for ADHD or bipolar disorder.[12]

Therefore, caregivers and professionals need to be very discerning before recommending pharmaceutical treatment. Recovery from child abuse is never as simple as prescribing a pill, and requires a multi-dimensional, long-term effort. Support, therapy, and especially love and acceptance, are critical for recovery. A peaceful home life, stability, approval and reassurance are of necessity to the extent possible, from family, caregivers, teachers and mentors.

Photo: www.istockphoto.com April Anderton

---

[12] Neven, R., et al., 1997.

Children with sleep disorders have also been mistakenly treated with medications for ADHD. Children who are having trouble sleeping are often misdiagnosed with ADHD.

There can be many reasons that children are having difficulty sleeping and there can be practical solutions as well. One counselor recommends a "wind down" period, one hour before going to bed. Also, keeping the television, video games and Internet out of the bedroom can be of help to many children. Making sure children do not view stimulating movies or play stimulating video games before bedtime can be of help. [13]

Children need exercise, as do adults. Healthy outdoor activities are demonstrated to help many children with symptoms of ADHD and depression, as well as being an aid in helping a child or adult to sleep better at night. [14]

Children often outgrow symptoms of ADHD

Of encouragement for parents of children with ADHD symptoms, is that up to 35%, some say 50% of children and teens who have the symptoms labeled as ADHD, outgrow these symptoms and no longer fall within a classifiable range. (Barkley, R., 2008, p.49).

Symptoms and behavioral issues may be most difficult for the teacher in the classroom, or sometimes for the parent, but ADHD seldom poses imminent danger to the child or to classmates.

Prevention:

Pregnant women who smoke, drink alcohol or abuse drugs put their future children at greater risk for ADHD. Good prenatal care, good diet when pregnant and regular visits to the doctor are essential. Breast feeding may also help the baby to bond with the mother and the mother to the baby, and this can be another effective preventive measure.

---

[13] Walker, S., 1998.

[14] Armstrong, T., 1997.

Chapter 2

The Media and ADHD?
Parental Training
Problems and Solutions
Diet
Media: Television, Movies, Video Games, Music

YOU AR GOING TO think about TV rather than egecation why You are in school.

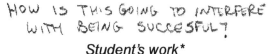

HOW IS THIS GOING TO INTERFERE WITH BEING SUCCESFUL?

Student's work*

"We must be willing to look at any and all aspects of a child's life that seem to be off-kilter and not just focus on the symptoms that are most apparent to adults. In my practice, I sometimes find that I can do the most good if I don't apply any diagnostic label at all." Scott M. Shannon, M.D., Pediatric Psychiatrist.

* reproduction

Studies indicate that children who play video games during school days have lower grades than children who do not. (Cummings, H., 2007, as reported in the Archives of Pediatrics and Adolescent Medicine. American Academy of Pediatrics).

Photo: Aaron Escobar

Excessive time watching television and movies has been shown, in some clinical studies, to have a correlational relationship with symptoms of ADHD in children. Content might also be a factor.

Television & Movies

The fast paced imagery of television, is said to have a connection, with a reasonable degree of certainty, with attentional problems. This is especially true with regards to young children. One study concluded that for every hour a day that a child watched television, his or her chances of manifesting the symptoms of ADHD as an older child increased by 18%.[15]

The content of what children watch also may have a bearing on their ability to concentrate. The Iman study on R-rated movies, violence and school grades, indicates that these are reversely correlated. The study concluded that children who watch R-rated movies, generally get lower grades.[16] Too much TV can also affect grades on math and reading scores.[17]

Violent films and television, as well as violent cartoons are being viewed by children as young as Kindergarten and pre-Kindergarten ages. In one classroom, 50% of first-graders watched films of extreme violence. For some, it has been noted, this can result in disorientation and inability to concentrate.[18] This observation has been noted in many classrooms. It is possible that long hours with television and movies might also contribute to symptoms of depression in some young children. (See: Remotely Controlled - How television is damaging our lives and what we can do about it, by Dr. Aric Sigman, pages 5, 187-189, 193).

Excessive time spent *with electronic stimuli*

Many children spend between 2 to 6.5 hours a day on the media, that is television, movies, video games, Internet, iPods, etc. The question is posed, "Are Our Children Too Wired?," in a Time magazine article. Many times, children or teens multitask, when watching TV, talking on the cell phone,

---

[15] Christakis D., et al, 2004.

[16] Imam, 2006.

[17] Parents Magazine, November 2005.

[18] New Jersey Teaching Notes, 2005-2010.

using the computer or iPod, making emails, (two or more activities at the same time).[19] Long hours with the media in any form can also contribute to symptoms of inattention, distractibility, and other symptoms associated with ADHD, and there seems to be evidence of a correlation between decreased performance in school in terms of lower grades with excessive time spent on electronic media such as television, movies and video games.[20]

Video Games

Boys especially can be susceptible to long hours daily on video games. Video games can be addictive for many children and teens. This might also contribute to symptoms associated with ADHD. (During a classroom discussion on anxiety, one teacher and counselor commented that children "don't really need video games," as fifth-grade students spoke of having two or three different types of video game units each.)[21] Parents can provide alternative, mentally, physically, healthful and enjoyable activities for children without needing to provide an assortment of mentally disorienting video games to children.

Roberto was 12 years old, he had been on medication for ADHD for over a year. Still, none of his teachers could handle him, and his parents didn't know what to do with him. His grades were still failing, and the child study team had tried a couple of different medications. However, a point that had never been addressed was that when Roberto came home from school, he didn't do homework or socialize, but usually played hours of the most-violent video games, unsupervised and alone. Is it possible that these many hours playing video games alone, might be affecting his ability to sit still in class, concentrate on schoolwork or to be able to integrate socially with other students? This illustrates the need to address root causes, rather than to emphasize treating symptoms, when considering childhood behavioral and mental health issues.

---

[19] Wallis, C., March 19, 2006.

[20] Cummings, H., 2007.

[21] New Jersey Teaching Notes, 2005-2010.

There are many options for entertainment that children often enjoy more than video games once they get used to the idea.

A school psychologist who had pre-teenage children of her own and who also regularly works with children who have symptoms of ADHD, says that after reading about the adverse psychological and possible adverse physical effects that video games can have on children and teenagers, took video games out of her home. Her children are of college age today and successful.[22]

Photo: Quinn Norton

Time spent with aggressive or violent video games might also have a correlation with symptoms of ADHD in some children.

---

[22] New Jersey Teaching Notes 2005-2010.

Movies

Some children watch between one and three movies daily, every day, or as many as five or six movies in a single weekend.[23] Fast-paced action movies and movies that feature the macabre or occult, scary, or horror movies, violent movies, can be overwhelming to the minds of children in their early childhood years.[24]

These can overwhelm the child's senses and leave them emotionally vulnerable, as well as make it difficult to concentrate on regular school work or "sit still" in class.[25] It has been noted that the effects of movies which have disturbing content are usually more intense with children who come from poorly structured families.[26]

Solutions

One educational psychologist, concerned with what she described as "the epidemic" of ADHD cases in her school, encouraged parents to set firm limits for children in terms of TV, video games and movies, as well as in other areas of life.[27] Parental training programs[28] have been recommended in an effort to help parents to fulfill their role, so they can learn to care for, direct, and in some cases, to learn how to raise and discipline children appropriately and effectively.

---

[23] New Jersey Teaching Notes, 2005-2010.

[24] Schmidt, B., 1991.

[25] Ibid.

[26] Neubauer, P., Ph.D.

[27] New Jersey Teaching Notes, 2005-2010.

[28] Hill, K., Ed.D. Paterson, NJ, 2005.

Benjamin Todd Jealous, president-elect, NAACP,
daughter, and wife Lia Jealous

*Children need firm limits and warm,
consistent personal attachments*

Parental Training

Parental training can be of much assistance to parents, by
teaching parenting skills. Parents can learn to help their children
through lifestyle adjustments, which can often lead to success in
the child's overcoming symptoms of ADHD.

Newly learned parenting skills can result in the child's
better coping with and even overcoming ADHD. The results may
well result in lightening the load on the parents themselves,
long run. Some community-based programs, as well as
programs from some religious organizations, and some public
schools, provide programs and seminars in parental training.
This can be of much value.

23

Keisha Hill, Ed.S., a school psychologist, states with compassion, "Every day I talk to hard-working educators, parents, guardians, and grandparents who are calling out for help in dealing with children with ADD/ADHD. Regarding the classroom, teachers and staff would benefit from training in research-proven strategies for children with ADD/ADHD.

Furthermore, from what I have seen, these strategies are potentially beneficial to all students, even those without attention difficulties. However, the school cannot create optimal environments for ADD/ADHD in isolation. The home environment is very important. Although many parents are doing the best they possibly can to help their inattentive/hyperactive child and to just make it through the day without a tantrum or crisis, parent training groups have proven to be very effective.

For example, once parents understand that children with attention difficulties cannot self-regulate or 'keep everything together' as well as other children, they will need assistance from a parent with concepts such as decision-making, time-management and organization." Parental training is a valuable provision for many parents and children that can make a big difference in a child's long-term success.

Music

Teens are often deeply enamored with music. It can become an almost religious passion. When this love for music is focused in a positive direction, it can provide wholesome recreation and contribute towards good mental health. For those who learn to play a musical instrument, for example, a child can gain a feeling of accomplishment and satisfaction, as well as self-esteem, as they make progress in developing their skills.[29]

---

[29] Timmes, A., 2005.

In some schools in Newark and Paterson, NJ, music teachers have programs whereby children can learn to play instruments such as the violin, something that children practice at home, and within six months time, most of the children in the public school program are playing very nicely. They are required to practice a half-hour a day at home, along with the time reserved for the activity a few times a week at school. Another middle school features piano lessons for their students, with 10 or 15 electric pianos made available for classes and practice.[30]

This can help children in their ability to focus and concentrate, as well as to develop a feeling of accomplishment and self-esteem. Similarly, while not necessarily scientifically proven at this point, children who are exposed to wholesome music from a young age might benefit in their cognitive ability and development. On the other hand, the intense music that dominates much of the music scene today, especially if youths or children overdo it in terms of intensity or time spent on this form of entertainment, can sometimes result in problems with inattention, depression, or contribute to the intensifying of some of the symptoms in some cases of bipolar disorder. There is what would seem to be, an established connection between intensity of music, in terms of its emotional impact, intensity and the amount of time spent, with some mental health difficulties. [32]

The amount of time spent with music is something that parents and mental health professionals, as well as educators and principals might need to give thought to also. Some schools have, in fact, incorporated strict policies in the school concerning ipod use and music during classes and in the halls. Moderation in music, then, can be part of the key for some teens. Exposing children and youth to music that is less intense, a wider variety of music that includes

---

[30] New Jersey Teaching Notes, 2005-2010.

[31] Robertson, J., 1998.

[32] Ibid, 1998.

exposure to lighter music such as light classical or other mood and folk music, can have a beneficial and positive effect on children.

For some children and youths who spend long hours with ipods, on the Internet with music, music videos and the radio, intensifying of symptoms associated with some childhood or teen mental health disorders might result. The mind is overwhelmed and cannot keep up with the intensity and fast pace that it is assimilating on a daily, even hourly basis. This, along with other factors, might contribute to symptoms of ADHD or depression in some children. ADHD may be the result of a genetic predisposition, along with any of a number of combinations of other factors, many of them controllable.

Learning to play a
musical instrument such as…

Violin or piano, can help a child to develop self esteem,[33] as well as to improve in his or her ability to concentrate.[34]

Photo: www.dreamstime.com Macromayer

---

[33] Timmes, A., 2005.
[34] New Jersey Teaching Notes, 2005-2010.

Chapter 3

Is Medication the Answer?
Drug treatment, Amphetamines
Note from Center for Disease Control and Prevention
Drugs have potential for abuse
Antidepressants
A realistic view of side effects

It is generally acknowledged in the psychiatric and psychological professional communities that medication treats symptoms, rather than the illness or the cause of the illness itself, in most treatment of psychiatric disorders for both adults and children.

The biggest reason parents are reluctant for their children to take medication for ADHD is the side effects. Some of those side effects can include, "insomnia, anorexia, nausea, decreased appetite, weight loss, headache, increased blood pressure, faster pulse, abdominal pain and shifting moods. In some people, stimulants may cause involuntary muscle movements of the face or body (tics)." At times, not commonly, they can cause more serious problems such as "seizures, high blood pressure (hypertension), delusions (psychosis) or liver problems." (Mayo Clinic, 2010).

Drug treatment, along with counseling and therapy, have typically been regarded as the front-line treatment for addressing ADHD (and depression) in the past 20 years or so. Treating adults and children with medication for mental health difficulties and disorders has been and continues to be the subject of much controversy and conflicting clinical studies. [35]

Stimulants are frequently prescribed for ADHD, and antidepressants have also become a secondary form of treatment when symptoms of depression become manifest in children. Symptoms of depression, after starting drug treatment for ADHD, does occur with some children. [36] It is possible that for some children, pharmaceutical treatment for ADHD might contribute to depression[37] or to symptoms of bipolar disorder over time. [38]

Medications for psychiatric disorders first came into mainstream use in the 1950s in psychiatric hospitals with the introduction of the drug commonly known as Thorazine, which was administered as an antipsychotic to acute patients. It is known as the first widely used typical antipsychotic. However it wasn't until the 1960s and early 1970s that psychiatric drugs for common mental health disorders became so popular. Only in the 1970s did drugs used for treating ADHD become widely used.

"...But the label—and the treatment—wouldn't have touched the true stress at the heart of Melanie's problem: her lack of connection with her overworked and emotionally unavailable parents." *Please Don't Label My Child, Scott Shannon, p.20*

---

[35] Kluger, J., 2003.

[36] Mental Health Weekly, 2004.

[37] MedTV, March 8, 2007.

[38] Shannon, S., 2006.

Drug Treatment for ADHD
Questions and Answers

Q - Do medications for ADHD have strong side effects?

A - Medications for ADHD in general do have strong side effects. Approximately 90% of those who take medications for ADHD will experience strong side effects when they initially take the drug. However, the intensity of the side effects gradually lessens, so that within six months, only 50% on the drugs will experience strong side effects, and by two years, only about 15% will. [39]

Q - What are the side effects of stimulant medications?

A - There are side effects in the use of the vast majority of prescription drugs. With every benefit comes a risk. Parents, treating physicians and child study teams, must evaluate risks vs. possible benefits. Some of the less serious side effects for medications used in treating ADHD are, changes in weight and eating habits, (stimulants act as an appetite suppressant - some other psychotropic drugs have the opposite effect and lead to weight gain or even diabetes), difficulty sleeping, changes in mood.

Other side effects that have been mentioned are, robotic effects, lack of flexibility, workaholic tendencies, insomnia, a feeling that you are going to "jump out of your skin". Facial tic-disorders and the exacerbation of previously occurring tic-disorders are relatively frequent side effects of stimulant medications. There are some reports of the development of Tourette Syndrome in association with the use of stimulant medications. [40]

---

[39] Rabiner, D. Attention Research Update newsletter.

[40] Mick, E. The relationship between stimulants and tic disorders in children treated for attention deficit hyperactivity disorder. *Harvard School of Public Health.*

College of the Ouachitas

Very serious side effects are experienced by less than 1% of those who take the drugs, and include, schizophrenic-like symptoms, suicidality, or sudden death due to heart failure for those (children) with undetected congenital heart defects. Side effects are the primary reason many parents are reluctant to prescribe medication for their children.

Q - Are there any who don't respond at all to ADHD medications?

A - About 40% of those who take medications for ADHD have no positive response. It seems to be a similar rate for antidepressants, where approximately 45% do not experience improvement for depression with antidepressant use.

Q - Are the positive effects of medications for ADHD long-term?

A - For those who experience positive effects from drugs for ADHD, those effects have a parallel profile to the side-effect curve. They are generally effective over the short term, but their effectiveness in individuals gradually lessens over one to two years.

Q - Do clinical studies support the use of non-pharmaceutical methods in treatment of ADHD?

A - Yes, there are some clinical studies which indicate that "green therapy," as one example, time spent outdoors in a natural setting, playing in the park, etc., does have a positive effect on symptoms associated with ADHD,[41] and can also have positive effects for depression and anxiety. Clinical studies do indicate that exercise is an effective natural therapy for depression, and that talk therapy for teens and some children does have benefit, and can also be a protective measure for some.

---

[41] Psychology Today, (March, April 2004).

Cognitive behavioral therapy for depression has been demonstrated to have a positive benefit at the same general rate as medication in the short-term, and is generally a better long-term solution. However, because pharmaceutical companies finance most of the studies being performed on the subject of treatment for mental health disorders, even those conducted by universities, there is a shortage of studies that have been conducted on non-pharmaceutical methods in the mental health field and in psychiatry in general.

Q - Do clinical studies support the view that medications for ADHD improve grades for children in school?

A - Results are mixed, but it has been concluded by some that grade performance is not significantly positively effected by medications for ADHD. Parents should not, then, expect dramatic improvement in grades through use of medications for ADHD. Parents, though, who are diligent in shielding children from negative media influences such as violence in the media, can expect positive gains in grade performance. [42]

Q - Does use of medications for ADHD lead to an increased risk of drug abuse?

A – While some medication advocates will say emphatically, No!, the answer appears to be up in the air at the present time. On the one hand, methylphenidate (Ritalin) and stimulants themselves are highly abused drugs. In some studies there may be indication that for the majority who use the drugs, it does not progress to abuse of illegal drugs at a disproportional rate.[43] On the other hand, some studies appear to contradict these findings. A study reported in the National Institute on Drug Abuse reported that in animal studies, rats which had been exposed to methylphenidate as juveniles develop a seven-times as great a rate of cocaine dependence as those which had not, as adults. The results of this study were not replicated for infant

---

[42] Cummings, 2007.

[43] Wilens, T.E., et al, 2003.

rats exposed to methylphenidate, which seemed to have close to the same rate of cocaine dependence. (Williams, J. Zickler, P., June 2003). The conclusion being that there may be some physical or psychological connection between adolescent exposure to some stimulant drugs and future drug use potential.

Amphetamines - Adderall *(Dextro/levo-amphetamine)* and Dexedrine *(Dextroamphetamine)* are amphetamines, widely prescribed for children in treatment for ADHD symptoms. Methylphenidate, most commonly prescribed as Ritalin, or in a long-lasting formula, Concerta, is the most well known medication for treating ADHD. Another medication that has been used is Cylert (pemoline) which is a long-lasting medication but that does not have the immediate affect of the amphetamines or of methylphenidate *(Ritalin)*. *(Reported cases of liver damage* has caused the FDA to issue warnings with the goal to phase Cylert out of use in the U.S.)* [44]

> *"There are several public health concerns relative to pharmacotherapy. Pharmacologic treatment is extremely prevalent. Assessing the health risks and benefits to young children, particularly preschoolers, is a high priority. Children who begin medication therapies very early and receive treatment on a long-term basis may have unknown risks associated with current treatments. Additionally, pharmacologic intervention often do not normalize behavior. Research, albeit limited, suggests that even with long-term treatment, children and adults with ADHD experience substantial problems in the school, home, workplace, and community settings. This raises questions about the effectiveness of pharmacologic interventions as a long-term approach."*
> Center for Disease Control and Prevention
> Department of Health and Human Services. US Government.
> (www.cdc.gov)

---

[44]   FDA Alert: Liver Injury Risk and Market Withdrawal, October 2005.

"Behavioral Modification" is one approach that is recommended by the *Center for Disease Control and Prevention for ADHD in children.*

******

Stimulants work by raising the dopamine level of the brain. Cocaine has a similar chemical structure to stimulant medications,[45] the difference being that cocaine is released rapidly, creating a rush, whereas stimulants are released gradually over a long and controlled period of time Therefore, the dopamine level is raised with stimulants, but not in the same rapid and addictive way as with cocaine.[46]

Drugs have potential for abuse and caution must be exercised by parents, educators and physicians. One can become psychologically or physically dependent on prescription medications. Methylphenidate and other stimulants are among the most widely abused drugs. Withdrawal symptoms of prescription medications can be severe. Both physicians and those taking amphetamines, as well as parents whose children may be taking amphetamines, need to be very cautious in their administering such drugs, as well as in protecting anyone in the household from abusing such prescribed drugs.

Methylphenidate is the fourth most widely abused drug today after marijuana, cocaine, and heroin, which are the top three. It is not necessarily the one to whom the drug is prescribed who is abusing it, although it can be, but the drug finds its way into the streets and is sold as a street drug or performance enhancer to college students.

"I have come to appreciate that medication ultimately treats symptoms, not problems," regarding psychiatric treatment. Psychiatrist Thad F. Ryals, MD

---

[45] Hallowell, E., Ratey, J., 1994.
[46] Medicating Kids: Interview with Russell Barkley. *PBS, Frontline*.

While it is commonly stated that 70% of those who take stimulant medications show improvement with drug treatment, it has been suggested that it is possible that much of the positive affect of drug treatment might be attributable to the therapy, support and attention that some children receive, in addition to the drug therapy, rather than being soley a result of the affect of the drug.[47]

The mere act of going to a doctor or even the attention from a caring nurse, a child's having someone that he or she can talk to about his or her situation, or that parents might be giving him or her more attention, is of benefit for many children. Additionally, there are few long-term studies concerning the effects of psychiatric medications on children and teens, including stimulant medications for ADHD. One comprehensive long-term study of ADHD treatment indicates that positive benefits of medication are negligible for most children within two years.[48] In other words, after taking the drugs for two years, stimulant medications no longer seem to make much of a difference for most children, although, children can become dependent on them for normal functioning.

Antidepressants

Antidepressants have been prescribed for over fifty years to treat depression. Tricyclic antidepressants, MAOIs, and more recently SSRIs such as fluoxetine (Prozac) and many others, are used by millions, both adults, teens and children. Presently, only Prozac has been approved for use in children. However, often, until a contrary ruling by the FDA for a particular drug, some doctors will prescribe many medications "off-label" to children, that is, outside of the FDA recommendation for the type of disorder the drug was intended or approved for.

Antidepressants have been used by many for help in overcoming symptoms of depression and for up to 50% of

---

[47] Placebo response is also very high in studies for ADHD.

[48] Attention Research Update, January 2006.

those who use them they have been of some help. There are many for whom antidepressants have not been of any value in overcoming depression and this might include up to approximately 45% of those who use antidepressants. The reasons for depression can be many and varied, therefore, it is to be expected that there would be different outcomes for different people.

The duration of the effectiveness of antidepressants varies from person to person. The expression, "Prozac Poopout," has been dubbed for the observation that there is a tendency for antidepressants to gradually or suddenly loose their effectiveness. This can happen within three to six months, or within a two to nine year period. For some, this can come in the form of a sudden crash, which can be intense and distressing.

Therefore, some psychiatrists and medical doctors have taken the viewpoint of using antidepressants only as a last resort in cases where there is a serious crisis in terms of danger to the client. The drug is used only as a temporary stop-gap until other issues such as lifestyle or trauma, that might be contributing to the depression, can be addressed, and never for more than a few months or as a lifestyle drug.[49]

Additionally clouding the issue with antidepressants, is that in recent studies, antidepressants are believed to be responsible for a doubled risk of suicidal thoughts in children and teens. This increased risk has been documented for those 18 to 24 years of age and possibly for some seniors. Presently, the only group that seems not to be vulnerable to increased risk of suicidality from antidepressant use is the 24 to 55 year old age group.[50]

"Very often medication treats symptoms only…" regarding the use of psychiatric medications in the treatment of various types of psychiatric disorders. Handbook of Clinical Neurobeahvioural Disorders. Jean Constantinidis and Jacques Richard, University Department of Psychiatry, Medical School of Geneva.

[49] Glenmullen, J., 2000; Shannon, S., 2007.
[50] Carey, B., 2007.

Also, some animal studies and one Dutch study seem to suggest that prolonged use of some antidepressants may be responsible for an increased rate of bleeding in the brain, and quadruples the risk of receiving a blood transfusion. All of the long-term physical effects of antidepressants in humans have not yet been determined.

The growing use of antidepressants and stimulants for young children, as early as preschool and kindergarten, is something of growing concern. Up to 10% of children are on psychiatric medications in some states (Virginia is one). A significant percentage of youths (adults and children) have been prescribed what are described as prescription "cocktails," that is, four, five or more different prescriptions prescribed at one time to achieve results, or to address various perceived issues.

Side effects are compounded with use of multiple medications. Some studies have concluded that there is no apparent benefit in the adding of more than one drug to a child or adult's drug regimen. [52]

Dr. George Albee, of the University of Vermont, was a prominent psychologist and former president of the American Psychological Association, and up until his recent death, wrote extensively on the subject of prevention and of the value of addressing social stressors in the diagnosis and treatment of mental health disorders. This, he felt, was especially true with regards to children. His view seemed to be that pharmaceuticals in the treatment of mental illness should not be used in treating children, and that it should not be emphasized with adults. [53]

---

[51] Kris L., et al., October 27, 2003.

[52] Sachs, G., 2007.

[53] Remembering George Albee. , 2006. *Society for Community Research and Action.*

For those who wish to stop using antidepressants, or any psychotropic drug, many sources indicate that they should do so gradually, rather than abruptly. Dr. Joseph Glenmullen is a psychiatrist who has written two books on the subject, Prozac Backlash and The Antidepressant Solution. Glenmullen describes his books as guides that can be used along with your doctor in an effort to successfully reduce an antidepressant prescription, with the goal of eventually doing without it.

Summary of serious side effect profile for stimulant medications

Serious side effects are possible with use of stimulant medications. The risk of serious side effects increases with the use of multiple medications. The percentage of children and youth who have serious side effects to stimulant medication decreases in time. Up to 90% will initially demonstrate what is considered to be serious side effects with use of medications commonly used in the treatment of ADHD symptoms. In six months time, the rate declines to about 50% and within two years on stimulant medications, the rate further decreases to around 15%. *(The rate of effectiveness for stimulant medications also seems to decline over the same period of time, almost proportionately to the side effect rate).*

About 40% will show no response to medication and around 5-10% are intolerant to any form of pharmaceutical treatment for ADHD. In the case of very serious side effects, such as schizophrenic-like symptoms, risk of suicide or sudden death due to heart failure, which has been reported with some stimulant medications, the rate is less than 1%.

---

[54] Kelly, R., 2005.

[55] Attention Research Update, 2006.

In the case of tic-disorders, stimulant medication has been demonstrated to result in increasing the risk of tic-disorders, that is, facial tics, in up to 9% of those who take stimulant medication.[56] Additionally, pre-existing tic-disorders can be exacerbated by the use of stimulant medications.

Tourette Syndrome has developed in a small number of children or youths who have begun stimulant medication treatment. In most cases, tic-disorders abate when treatment is suspended.[57]

A recent study concluded that methylphenidate may increase hostility and possibly aggression in children who take the drug for ADHD symptoms.[58]

Additionally, forcing or coercing a child to take medication is something that is not recommended by a number of mental health professionals.[59] This can cause some children to become rebellious, resentful, or cause a teen to distance themselves emotionally from a parent. Two noted psychiatrists and experts in the field of ADHD explain that children should never be forced to take medication, but only if they do so of their own volition, as this could be damaging in the long term.[60]

*On the effectiveness of psychoeducation intervention in mental health treatment, Fahriye Oflaz PhD, Sevgi Hatipolu PhD and Hamdullah Aydin MD similarly state in a paper published in the Journal of Clinical Nursing, that psychiatric "medication treats symptoms." ***

---

[56] Wilens, T., et al., 2006. Archives of Pediatric and Adolescent Medicine.

[57] Mick, E. The relationship between stimulants and tic-disorders in children treated for attention deficit hyperactivity disorder. *Harvard School of Public Health*.

[58] King, S., et al., 2008.

[59] Mate, G., 1999.

[60] Hallowell, E., Ratey, J., 1994.

* The specific disorders that the paper was addressing were depression and post traumatic stress disorder, (PTSD) but the princple also applies to ADHD.

Chapter 4

Other Solutions
Green therapy
Exercise
Art, Professional Art Therapy
Love

Questions to ask

- *What, if anything, seems to worsen symptoms?*
- *What, if anything, seems to help in diminishing symptoms?*

******

"As an art educator with AD/HD, I have been both a student with AD/HD, and a teacher of students with AD/HD. In the public schools [and at the college level], the art room is often the one place where others with AD/HD feel at home. The point is that when kids with AD/HD find [or create] an environment supportive of their needs, the AD/HD becomes a non-issue, and in some cases, an asset. By harnessing their creative energy and finding a productive outlet for their intelligence, the possibilities are endless. The potential for success and the enjoyment of life is enormous! To those with AD/HD, I recommend flipping the coin and embracing what you find on the other side." Daniella Barroqueiro, Ph.D., Illinois State University, 2006

Are There Other Treatment Solutions to Symptoms of ADHD?

Yes. Some have found success in reducing the amount of time spent watching television, movies and video games to the greatest extent possible. The conclusion of one special education teacher who commented succinctly on her view of children's behavioral and attentional difficulties in school was, that most students had difficulty concentrating because of *"the media"*. The average time spent on the media for children and teens is between 2 ½ to 6 ½ hours a day. (In the school in which she worked, one girl reported that her sister played up to 16 hours in one day on video games). That rate actually has increased, according to the most recent reports, by as much as 15% since this statistic of 2 1/2 to 6 1/2 hours was reported in 2005.

- One father with a large family took the step of keeping video games put away during school months.[60]

- One parent limited television time to one-half hour a day for her young children, while providing other forms of wholesome recreation for the children, along with encouragement for the children to spend more time reading. Another parent does not allow cable television in his home (he lives in a region where only cable TV is available) because of the violence that is common in programming for children. [61]

  Taking the television and video games (as well as open access to the Internet) out of the bedroom of a child or teen can also be of value for many for many who have attentional difficulties.

- One father whose son was struggling with attentional problems and whose grades were suffering as a result, took the step of allowing children to watch TV and play

---

[60]   New Jersey Teaching Notes, 2005-2009.

[61]   Ibid.

video games only on the weekends during school months. While the children were reportedly a little antsy the first two weeks, soon, the time they had spent with TV and video games became filled with outdoor activities, playing together and reading. The improvement in school work and ability to read and concentrate was nothing short of remarkable. The boy achieved the honor-role within six months. He had received a few months of tutoring prior to that. Previously, he had difficulty doing the simplest math problems for his age group and was at least a year behind in his math. [63]

What About Diet?

One reading coach who works with learning disabled children, including children who display the symptoms of ADHD, says that the first thing she encourages parents to do is to take their children off of a diet high in refined sugar. [64] It is possible that a poor diet might contribute to the intensity of some symptoms for some children with ADHD, or it may be a contributing factor for some of the symptoms, according to a spokesperson for CHADD. [65]

However, it seems to be unlikely that a high sugar diet or diet alone causes ADHD, but rather, it seems more likely that diet may be one of a number of contributing or aggravating factors. A vigorous meta-analysis of the effects of sugar on children's behavior and cognition concluded that, while such did not cause significant behavioral problems, "a small effect of sugar on subsets of children cannot be ruled out." (Wolraich, M. L., L, M.D., et.al., 1995). Adjusting to a more nutritious diet, then, for a child, can be a good and simple first or second step that parents take.

---

[63] Ibid.

[64] McNuff, J., 2005. Paterson, NJ.

[65] Phone Interview, 2005.

Obesity and problems associated with it among children is also of concern to many professionals and parents in recent years. In India approximately 10% of all children are reported to be obese, with a correspondingly higher rate of diabetes.

Food additives may affect the mood or behavior of some children. Parents, though, should realize that it is rarely one factor that is causing a child to lack in his or her ability to concentrate, but it is usually a combination of factors. Focusing on something narrow such as food additives might prove to be frustrating rather than constructive, so when it comes to diet, parents need to be balanced. Some food additives which are mentioned with reference to ADHD are benzoate, FD&C Yellow No.6 (sunset yellow), FD&C Yellow No.1 (quinoline yellow), FD&C Yellow No.5 (tartartrazine), FD&C Red No. 40 (allura red). (Huxsahl, J.E., M.D., Mayo Clinic). If food additives are a real concern to some parents, they might consider purchasing only organic foods, which some do for a number of reasons. Organic food can typically add approximately 35% to the grocery bill.

Children need breakfast, as this can affect their ability to concentrate in school. However, sugary cereals can work in the opposite direction for some children, whose metabolism might be sensitive, and cause them to lose the ability to concentrate well, as there is little nourishment in most sugary cereals. A healthy breakfast is a must for both young children and teenagers whose bodies are rapidly developing.

A low sugar diet by avoiding sugars found in sugary cereals, soda, chocolate, and flavored milk,[66] candy, ice cream, cakes, sugary juices, etc., can be of some help for general health, weight loss, and a more active lifestyle, as well as for a child's ability to concentrate. Schools may want to consider upgrading the quality of the food provided for children by replacing sugary breakfasts and snacks with more nutritious foods and foods that have a lower sugar content. This could prove to be beneficial in terms of the diabetes rate among children, as well as in teaching children through example how to eat healthfully.

---

[66] Chocolate and strawberry milk are served to children at school, and are loaded with added sugar.

In an effort to remedy this problem, a number of schools and parents' groups have worked together in formulating more nutritious meals for children, [67] which can significantly contribute to better classroom performance and behavior. Natural snacks such as fruit, wholewheat crackers with little added sugar, raw vegetables and other natural foods are a healthy alternative to high sugar snack foods. All of this can be of value in two ways to children. First it will help them to concentrate better in class, their sugar level will remain more constant, and their chances of developing diabetes as children or teens will be diminished. [68]

Second, it will help children to establish good life patterns, not just by what they read in textbooks, but by a positive example that is set in school in good nutrition.

A note on depression: The reasons for childhood depression, like ADHD, are many and varied, and every child is wired differently, but these are a few things that parents and professionals can be aware of. Trauma both present and past, can contribute to depression. A death in the family or of a loved one can affect a child's mental health. Excessive time with movies can affect the mental health of children. Violence in the media may be a contributing factor to some children, as may the quantity and type of music a child or teenager listens to. (Robertson, J.) Some popular music for children can be emotionally intense and overload on music which is deeply emotional may affect the mood of some children and teens. Diet might also be a contributing factor for some childhood depression, and children do benefit from regular exercise and "fresh air". For some children, love and attention are the real prescription that no drug or medicine can replace. Love is an essential element for good mental health. Talk therapy, or interpersonal therapy, helps many children and teens. Cognitive behavioral therapy also is of value in treating depression in children, teens and adults.

---

[67] Moody, S., 2007.

[68] A high sugar diet, such as is served in many school breakfasts, can contribute to diabetes.

Green Therapy

Richard Louv's recent book with a theme described in terms of "Nature Deficit Disorder" relates that children have experienced a serious decrease in the amount of time spent in natural surroundings. His book was written in an effort to help raise awareness for the positive effects that "green time" can have on children, who might otherwise become detached from the natural world. [69]

Photo: www.istockphoto.com   Monkey Business Images

Outdoor activities and exercise, when regular, can help many children with ADHD or depression.

Psychology Today reported that children who spend time in the outdoors exercising or playing experience a marked decrease in symptoms of ADHD. [70]   This can be true for symptoms associated with depression also. [71]

---

[69]   Lugara, J., October 2004.

[70]   Psychology Today, March /April 2006.

[71]   Heliq, 2007.

44

One study by Duke University indicated that exercise proved to be more beneficial in treatment of mild to moderate depression than medication, in terms of both recovery and recurrence rate. Further, the study indicated that exercise alone was surprisingly more efficacious in treating mild to moderate depression than medication along with exercise, both in efficacy, as well as in a reduction of recurrence rate.[72] The reason exercise alone may be more efficacious than exercise combined with medication, in terms of long-term recovery rates in moderate depression, might be because the mind gets used to the medication, and when you try to stop, it can leave you more vulnerable to relapses of symptoms. This can especially be the case if underlying issues have not been fully addressed.

Exercise

When one youth who had been diagnosed with ADHD began attending the gym daily with his father, it proved to be of value to him in controlling symptoms of ADHD. Additionally, his mother, who works in education, stated that having more structure in the household was of much value to her son. A regular, set time to eat and sleep, as well as a regular daily routine, along with exercise, helped her son to overcome some of the symptoms of ADHD, to the point that medication, the side effects of which were uncomfortable for her son, was no longer needed.[73]

Many children with symptoms of ADHD are visually-oriented. Directing that predisposition positively by parents and teachers, away from highly stimulating video games, movies and television, and rechanneling that strength towards art, can help children settle down in class and in their schoolwork.

---

[72] Awake, January 8, 2002.

[73] New Jersey Teaching Notes, 2005-2009.

Exercise and "green time," as simple as walking a mile a day, is believed to be more effective in treating moderate depression than medication, both in short-term and in long-term efficacy. It also can be an effective therapy for ADHD.

http://www.istockphoto.com kzenon

Think Green--

Regular outdoor activities such as...

Playing in the park
Hiking
Camping
Jumping Rope
Biking
Skating
Skateboarding
Brisk Walking
Jogging

...can help children to overcome the symptoms associated with ADHD and depression.

Art can strengthen the mind, can train a child to concentrate for an extended period of time on one subject and can provide children with a wholesome pastime that is pleasing to the eyes. Regular art lessons can help a child to develop a love for art and to stick with it. This can help a child to develop a longer attention span, to learn to concentrate and to sit still. Art is an important skill and therapy for children with ADHD symptoms.

Art can really make a difference. It not only helps a child to learn to concentrate, but also helps to build self-esteem, which is something that can be lacking with some children who have ADHD or other disabilities. Art can instill creativity and satisfy a child's need for visual stimulation in a gentle way, and at the same time, it can help to take the child's attention away from the TV, movies and video games, which may be part of the core reasons behind some children's inability to focus, or that may be contributing to a child's hyperactivity.

Art lessons can be an excellent investment in a child's time. Trips to art galleries are a nice outing for children. Some public schools have murals which children and teenagers have painted or are painting on the school walls in the hallways. It is an application of the use of art in the school system that is both positive and that enhances school morale. It is also a good project for children in special education, for children with special needs, to be involved with.

Very simply, replacing a child's TV, movie and video game time with art can make a big difference.

"It's our job to listen to them attentively and openly, to resist labeling them, and to work to remove the stressors from their lives that are blocking their mental and emotional health." Scott M. Shannon, M.D.

.

---

[74] Barroqueiro, D., Ed.D., 2006.

Children who end up being labeled ADHD often are very visually-oriented. When this is channeled positively towards art, then that liability turns into a positive, with increased potential for creativity and productivity.

Some Art Resources for Children and Teens:

Drawing on the Right Side of the Brain,
by Betty Edwards. Great book!

Drawing With Children
By Mona Brookes
Tarher, Perigee 1986, LA.

Encouraging the Artist in Your Child
By Sally Warner
St. Martin Press, NY 1989

Drawing Faces - Usborne Art Ideas
By Jan McCafferty
E.D.C. Publishing, 2002

Art Junction: http://www.artjunction.org/young.php
Art Education, Program of University of Florida
Art junction is described as a collaborative site for teachers and students. It has good information with details on teaching art to children, at various stages, including preschoolers, and how to nurture their creative ability, along with some specifics on what materials are best to use. Recommended. It has resources for teachers, teens and children, as well as helpful links.

Something Different: www.youdraw.com *is a website where you can draw your own pictures on an electronic pad on the computer, which are posted onto the site. It is something children can do so that their works get some kind of viewing audience. The images are to be published in a book, so their drawings may appear in print, which also is something positive for children.*

Two good sites to learn to draw portraits:
About.com
http://drawsketch.about.com/od/drawingportraits/Portrait_Drawing_Faces.htm
Portrait Artist.org
http://www.portrait-artist.org/face/

Professional Art Therapy

Professional Art Therapy is a real and growing branch of psychology. Art therapists are board certified and are located throughout the United States. *The American Art Therapy Association* can educate you on this non-alternative form of therapy in treating many mental health disorders in children, teens, and adults.

American Art Therapy Association (AATA).
www.arttherapy.org
The AATA represents approximately 5,000 members and 36 AATA state and regional chapters that conduct meetings and activities to promote art therapy on the local level.

Magazine Ideas for Children:

* Big Backyard
* Animal Baby
* Ranger Rick

National Wildlife Federation
http://www.nwf.org
800-822-9919

* Faces Magazine
Cobblestone & Cricket

Very nice magazine
for children ages 9-14
www.cobblestonepub.com

photo page 56 : www.istock.com: Arnie Pastoor

Children need time,
attention, approval and LOVE

Children and ART- A healthy mix and natural "cure" for ADHD

Love - One of our greatest emotional and
psychological needs is love. Without love, psychological problems are bound to increase. Love is a healer. It has been described as "the best prescription". Many children who have symptoms of ADHD do come from very loving families and homes. This gives such children a wonderful edge to cope with the difficulties that accompany symptoms of ADHD.

Many children who have been abused often may manifest the symptoms of ADHD, and a disproportional number of children from single family homes are diagnosed.[75]

---

[75] Neven, et al., 1997.

Children need unconditional love, as well as the approval of their parents, teachers and from others. Parents need to spend time with their children, to help them with their homework, to establish loving but firm boundaries and to protect them from harmful influences. This takes time and effort. The television or the unsupervised Internet are not good babysitters. They can be tools of "isolation and distraction," [76] as one grade school teacher commented in a letter to the parents of her students. Another educator and special education student said of her preschool students, with concern and some frustration, "these children don't need medicine, they need patience and love." [77]

A teacher never knows what a child may be going through at home, so must learn to deal with children and teenagers in their care patiently and lovingly, as many do.

A parent or teacher who is critical can damage a child's self-esteem, which can contribute to problems later in life. Any activity that bolsters self-esteem can be part of the healing effort for children with ADHD symptoms.

Some teachers and principals, truly are a source of love towards children of all ages, and it is heartwarming to see. Parents need to be patient with children and to give them their love, attention and approval, which can be a challenge when raising children with special needs. The constant berating or cruelly ridiculing a child can be considered to be a form of child abuse. Children need to be reasoned with and helped to understand the hows and whys of a certain action or conduct rather than be forced or bullied.

---

[76] Booker, K. 2004. Letter, Paterson, NJ.
[77] Communication, Teaching Notes, 2005, Paterson, NJ.

Avoiding overburdening yourself with guilt

Parents also need to be merciful to themselves and should avoid overburdening themselves with guilt. Such thoughts as, "What did I do wrong? Why didn't I act sooner? If only we had...," accomplish little and only add to the burden of a parent. The decision of whether or not to use medication can be an agonizing one for many parents and at times, it is a decision that can divide a family.

Guilt can wear a family down. By dealing with the present, looking forward rather than backward, and doing everything you can do now rather than dwelling on the past, you can develop a positive, forward looking attitude that is solution-oriented. If there were mistakes made, it should be remembered that "life is about making mistakes and learning from them." By addressing lifestyle changes, this can result in solutions and a better life for the child and family. No family, no parents and no children are perfect. We can't expect perfection of ourselves or or from any of our children. We need to maintain balance and a positive attitude towards our children. One mother whose daughter had been diagnosed with ADHD said that she had to work hard to maintain a positive attitude towards her daughter.[78]

Doing this will be reflected in the way we speak and treat our child, and result in a better long-term relationship with him or her. If we believe in the children and maintain hope, this will be demonstrated in our tone of voice and conduct towards the child, and the child will pick up on this. This will help the child, in turn to see themselves positively, and not to give up when difficulties arise in their life and circumstances, which will happen at one time or another. *Never give up. "Love hopes all things."*

---

[78] Timmes, A., 2005.

52

Chapter 5

Educational Solutions

Workable Solutions from within the School System
Educational Remediation
One-on-one Attention
Specific Teaching Techniques
18 Positive Educational Ideas
Mentoring, Tutoring
Coaching, Coaching Resources
Reading
Conclusion

"Many elementary school children rated by their teacher as having clinically significant inattentive symptoms, do not show similar problems the following year." David Rabiner, Ph.D., and associates, in a recent study of children with attentional difficulties, published in the Journal of Developmental and Behavioral Pediatric, April 2010.

"Various explanations are possible including positive change in the child associated with maturation, the resolution of a significant life stressor, or perhaps improved nutrition and/or sleep. Teachers may also use rating scales differently, with some teachers prone to assign higher ratings than others.

However, it is also possible that for some children, a change in classroom context is an important factor. This echoes findings obtained with middle school students, where ratings of ADHD symptoms between teachers often do not show strong agreement. This difference has been attributed by some researchers to the unique characteristics associated with different classrooms."

Workable solutions from within the school system

www.dreamstime.com   Nyul

Educational Remediation

Some   have found that good results can be achieved by making simple lifestyle changes and by making   use of educational tools or techniques   that helps make concentration easier for children. Dr. Susan Ashley, a clinical psychologist with many years of experience, who works with children with special needs daily, recommends educational remediation and therapy rather than medication as a frontline   defense for ADHD. This can   accomplish much for a child. [79]

---

[79]   Ashley, S., Ph.D., 2005.

One-on-One Attention

Many children with learning disorders, especially those without fathers, benefit from individual one-on-one attention. Instructional assistants are available in some situations and this can be of help for some children. Big Brother programs are an option. One substitute teacher in a large inner city said that what he valued most about his work was his ability to be a positive role model and father-figure to fatherless boys.

After-school tutoring to help children or teens with reading or other subjects may also be available through schools[80] or through public libraries [81] and some after-school programs, and this has also helped many.

Both the practical attention to reading, as well as the stability and safe haven created through the one-on-one attention are of help and stabilizing to children.

School psychologists and social workers can listen to children who might have deep-rooted problems due to abuse or trauma. A good support team does make a difference. Mentors from various programs, both educational, and through community and religious-based programs,[82] such as personal, supervised bible study, can be of help for some fatherless boys and girls with emotional problems, and for some children with symptoms associated with ADHD. But especially, parents should take time to give one-on-one attention to their children.

Read with your child, take time to talk to him or her, put them to bed and read to them at night, help them with their homework. Don't delegate parenting to others, but find joy in your active role as a parent, or in some cases, grandparent or guardian.

---

80   Reading Recovery. www.readingrecovery.org.
81   McNuff, J., 2005. Paterson, NJ.
82   New Jersey Teaching Notes, 2005-2009.

Some specific teaching techniques that can be helpful:

- Use of visual aids and pictures - Children with ADHD symptoms are often highly visual, as are many children today. One professional estimate is that 80% of today's children are visually-oriented.

- Breaking larger assignments into smaller tasks can help.

- Some teachers have found that seating children with attentional problems close to the teacher's desk and within eye contact is helpful. Careful attention to seating arrangements in general can also be of value.

- A buddy system, where progressive and well-adjusted students team up with students who have learning difficulties has proven to be an effective way of both helping the struggling student, and in teaching students who are in a position to give, to find joy in helping others.

"When you hear the word ADD, the next word that follows is medication. 75-80% of those who are diagnosed with ADHD will at some point be prescribed medication. "Why the push for medication? Why not urge for parent training, specialized classrooms and social skills training? We can hypothesize why parents are are pressured. Medication is relatively inexpensive, highly profitable, easy to give and takes almost no effort. Parenting is a tough job. 'If a pill can make your job easier, why not? We need to ask, 'What can I do instead?" (condensed for brevity)
Susan Ashley, Ph.D., Clinical Psychologist - *ADD & ADHD Answer Book - The Top 275 Questions Parents Ask.*

---

* Some of the ideas on this page and the following pages are adapted from Sandra Reif's book, How to Reach and Teach ADD/ADHD Children (1987).

18 Positive Educational Ideas
that can be of value for children with symptoms of ADHD

*1. **Work with children on an individual level, one-on-one one.** Children with special needs benefit from one-on-one attention. Provide mentors or instructional assistants, or enroll a child in after-school tutoring.*

*2. **Clarity and structure** - Clear step-by-step instructions help children with attentional difficulties to focus.*

*3. **Creative, engaging, pro-active teaching** is of importance for children with symptoms of ADHD.*

*4. **School psychologists, as part of a support team, can be of help.** Additionally, social workers in the public schools and substance abuse counselors have increasingly taken on the role usually reserved for psychologists. They, too, have become a vital link for struggling children and youth.*

*5. **Parental training** - Educating parents, parental training, has been recommended as a part of a school effort to help children by helping the parents and family.[83] Some public school principals have arranged for informative parental training sessions for parents of children in their school. Some local community programs and religious organizations also feature various forms of parental and family training.*

*6. **Open communication between school and family is of importance.** This requires effort on the part of both teachers and parents.[84]*

*7. **Positive reinforcement** - Focus on the positive and build on it with your children, (at home and in school), rather than belittling or ridiculing.*

---

[83] Hill, K, Ed.D 2005, Paterson, NJ.

[84] Family therapy can also be a supportive therapy and can add to the effectiveness of other interventions.

8. Improving one's teaching style and dedication to help children can help some children to focus better in the classroom. Many children with symptoms associated with ADHD need nurturing. Young children are affected emotionally and psychologically from disruptions in family life such as separation or divorce, so teachers need to take these social and family issues into consideration in dealing moderately with children whose behavior is not consistent.

9. Encourage children to write regularly in a journal.
This can be an effective way to get a hold on negative emotions. Some teens find writing poetry to have an emotionally healing effect.

10. Breaking down larger tasks into smaller tasks in the classroom can help many children with short attention spans to accomplish tasks and complete their assignments.

11. Extensive use of graphics, color and pictures
helps all children to focus and concentrate on their school work, as well as to retain more information, but this is especially true of children with symptoms of ADHD.

12. Attention to seating in class for children with learning and attentional problems is of some help for many children with learning difficulties and can be of help for the teacher.

13. Use of relaxing and subdued music in class helps children to keep calm and focus. Some schools are strict in their rules concerning ipods in class, in the halls and at school. Constant music while a child or teen does his schoolwork, or in off-minutes, can prove to be extremely distracting and "fragment" the mind and thinking of a child, making it difficult for him or her to concentrate on assignments requiring a high degree of cognitive skill. Principals need to be aware of how ipod music during the school day at school, can lead to a lower level of academic achievement in many children and teens and might also contribute to behavioral problems. Parents need also to be aware of this.

14. ***Regularly assigning homework*** *helps children to engage in positive activities after school, rather than in spending too much time on video games or television. In addition to the learning aspect of the assignment, it helps to strengthen the mind and attention span of the child. Many grade school teachers regularly assign one to two hours of homework per day. This is of value in helping children to develop academically, and in teaching them a good work ethic.*

15. ***Classroom buddies*** *from among excelling students can be of much value. This has something of a positive effect in both directions, for the child who needs help, and for the child who is giving the assistance.*

16. ***Attentive teaching assistants*** *can be of value in both special education and in regular classrooms.*[85]

17. ***Give both oral and written directions to children.*** *Some students might do better with oral-testing rather than with written-testing. Many students excel when pro-active teaching methods are used such as question and answer, but might not do well when given a textbook reading and writing assignment. Different aptitudes and different types of learning styles can be taken into consideration when dealing with children with special needs or who have symptoms of ADHD.*

18. ***Keep movies out of the classroom.***
Movies are not such a good time-filler for children in school. Excessive TV and movie viewing, especially as a lifetime habit, can contribute to lazy mental and life-habits as well as to obesity, a growing problem among children in many cultures. Choose art over movies. Many movies today are generally fast-paced, many have macabre themes. It is of note that after movie-time in school, it may take a long time for some children to "wind down" and concentrate again on school work. (This is referring to non-educational films for entertainment, in contrast to many educational videos which have much value in education.)

---

[85] New Jersey Teaching Notes 2005-2010.

Movies in School

One of the contributing factors towards developing ADHD symptoms for children may be overdoing it with movies. If anything, schools should discourage rather than encourage movies in school. This is especially in view of the fact that young children are indulging in movies of various degrees of violence, and that many popular children's movies are violent, very intense, or have scenes of violence or shocking violence. Schools can unwittingly or tacitly reinforce that life-pattern for many children.

Many teachers, substitute teachers, and teaching assistants, as well as schools in general, use entertaining movies with marginal or no educational value as regular time-fillers.

Character education has proven to have much value in the public school system and in the classroom. Many classrooms have lessons, words and ideas featuring positive values and ideas posted on the walls and on posters in the school and classroom.[86] In some schools, students paint positive quotes on the hallway and stairwell walls. It helps to create an atmosphere conducive to learning, good conduct and positive values.

However, the lessons to be learned from a large percentage of movies for children, even in the classroom, and what children are generally watching at home, often present the opposite message.[87] Revenge, win at all costs, might makes right, or delight in other's suffering may be the underlying themes. Further, fast-paced movies and cartoons, which might have scenes of violence and intensity, may be a part of the root of many attentional problems for some children. Using movies regularly in public grade schools, may be contributing to a lower quality of education, but it might also be teaching life lessons passivity rather than active participation. This might have broader implications for society as a whole. Movies in class can make it more difficult for a child or teen to focus on classwork other times during the day.[88]

---

[86] New Jersey Teaching Notes, 2005-2009.

[87] Ibid.

[88] Ibid.

Rather, teaching positive life-skills such as helping young people to appreciate art for recreation and pleasure, encouraging young people and children to learn to play a musical instrument or write poetry, attachment to some recreational sport, to enjoy and appreciate the outdoors, can help a child or teen to mature emotionally and develop a positive set of values.

It has been noted that children who manifest the symptoms of ADHD need support. They need caring, loving, but firm parents and guardians. They need to know what their proper bounds are and they also need consistency. That takes time and effort and there have been some innovative efforts along this line. One educator found a successful formula in teaching his students, all of whom had symptoms of ADHD, in a classroom that allowed more spontaneity and creativity. Many children with special needs, including ADHD, respond well with one-on-one attention.

Tutoring, Mentoring and Coaching

Tutoring, mentoring and coaching can prove to be of benefit for many children with symptoms of ADHD. The ADDA Association recommends coaching for children with ADHD.

A coach is not a therapist or doctor, it is someone who has been trained to help an adult, child or teenager with the practical areas of life which may be difficult to deal with symptoms of ADHD. Coaching is a tool that is being used by many for both mental health disorders and in other areas of life. The cost of coaching is less than that of a therapist, and there are organizations that can provide a list of coaches in your area. Coaches work in harmony with the psychologist or therapist.

Some who may not be receptive to other forms of treatment or therapies may show a positive response to coaching. Coaches may work by phone, webcam, some may work in person, or use a combination of these approaches. A coach might speak to a client daily for 15 minutes, or at other scheduled times for longer periods.

A good coach will provide encouragement and give reinforcing advice on how to keep one's life organized, how to make lifestyle changes and to stick to one's recovery plan.

Coaching can help adults, teens and even children. Like anything, care must be taken to choose a coach that fits into your style and one that both you and your child or teen get along with. For adults with ADHD, psychotherapy, marital counseling, family therapy and coaching, are some of the possible ways of addressing some issues. Support groups can also be of help to some adults or parents.

Coaching Resources:

IAAC
www.adhdcoachinstitute.org

ADHD Coaches Organization
www.adhdcoaches.org

ICF
www.coachfederation.org

ADHD Coach Academy
www.addcoachacademy.com

Reading

Teaching children to enjoy reading for pleasure and learning is a valuable skill and life-lesson to impart. Children who read rather than watch too many hours of television, develop powers of concentration and are better equipped to be successful in their education. [89] One professional reading coach stated that "one of the greatest tragedies of this world is that children no longer know how to sit down alone and find pleasure in reading a good book." [90] Teach your child or student to appreciate the value of reading. Reading, without iPod, music and noise, can be refreshing to the mind and soul.

---

[89] Wall Street Journal, 2007.

[90] McNuff, J., 2005. Paterson, NJ Public Library.

Neurofeedback and Biofeedback

Neurofeedback can be likened to exercise for the mind. It is high-tech, can be costly, but in reality, a cost analysis between the long-term cost of medication in comparison to that of neurofeedback might be comparable. Both biofeedback and neurofeedback involve attaching electrodes to the head or other parts of the body which are measured to give feedback on the brain activity, or that of other parts of the body. In the case of biofeedback, that also might include areas of skin, heart, and so on. Neurofeedback deals only with the central nervous system.

These should only be performed professionally, after a thorough examination and by a licensed, trustworthy practicioner. While not as widely accepted as some other forms of treatment, there is evidence that neurofeedback can be effective.

A child or adult can learn to develop ability to concentrate and focus through neurofeedback, and both neuro and biofeedback are being applied to a wide range of mental health and other disorders, including anxiety, bipolar disorder, OCD, epilepsy, alcoholism and drug abuse.

It is not so mysterious as it might seem at first, and is simply a way to learn to control one's mind, and in the case of biofeedback, body functions. It can be used along with other forms of therapy and self-help measures.

While more research is needed, neurofeedback has become a somewhat accepted form of treatment, a more or less mainstream approach to treating ADHD and some other disorders.

Biofeedback/Neurofeedback Resources

What is Neurofeedback?, by D. Corydon Hammond, Ph.D.
http://www.isnr.org/uploads/whatisnfb.pdf

The Association for Applied Physiology and Biofeedback
www.aapb.org

The International Society for Neurofeedback & Research
www.isnr.org

Also, New York Biofeedback Services has some good information.
www.nybiofeedback.com

Chapter 6

Resources

Helpful References
Mental Health Checklist for Parents and Educators
Charts and Graphs
Bibliography
Index

Helpful References

ADD & ADHD Question and Answer Book, 2005. Susan Ashley, Ph.D., clinical psychologist who works with children. She leans towards advocating non-pharmaceutical interventions for ADHD as a frontline strategy.

Attention Research Update
www.helpforadd.com
email to subscribe: attentionresearchupdate@helpforadd.com
One of the most well-researched newsletters and websites on ADHD.
> David Rabiner, Ph.D., Senior Research Scientist
> Center for Child and Family Policy
> Duke University, Durham, NC

The Antidepressant Solution, 2007 by Dr. Joseph Glenmullen
A Step by Step Guide to Safely Overcoming Antidepressant Withdrawal, Dependence and Addiction. See also, Prozac Backlash.

Are We Giving Kids Too Many Drugs? Medicating Young Minds. November 3, 2003. *Time Magazine.*[91]

Note: Able Child is a grass roots type of child advocacy organization, similar in its genre to M.A.D.D. (Mother's Against Drunk Driving), that provides assistance for parents who feel they are being pressured or forced by school systems for their child to take medication for ADHD. Non-profit. www.ablechild.org

Bipolar Children, 2007. Edited by Sharna Olfman, Ph.D.
describes the overdiagnosis of bipolar disorder in children, the overmedicating of children who are labeled "bipolar," and some of the reasons for this. Excellent documentation of a serious issue.

---

[91] Vincent Iannelli, M.D., author and website counselor (About.com), who sometimes supports medications for children, states, *"this article does a fairly good job of describing the risks vs. benefits of treatment."*

Blaming the Brain: The Truth About Drugs and Mental Health,
1998. Elliot Valenstein, PhD. Looks at the history of psychiatric
treatment, and presents evidence that mental illness is not like
diabetes, high blood pressure or heart disease. Valenstein disagrees
with the medical model of mental health, and the opinion that "chemical
imbalances" cause mental health disorders or that pharmaceuticals can
cure them. Valenstein is professor emeritus of psychology and
neuroscience at Michigan State University.

Lead Poisoning - NJ Department of Community Affairs

101 South Broad St.
Trenton, NJ 08625
www.leadsafenj.org
877-DCA-LEAD
(Contact the appropriate agency in your own state if you suspect lead
poisoning)

Lead poisoning (and other environmental contaminants, are a
contributing factor in 2 to 10% of cases of ADHD in the United
States, according to the research of Joel Nigg, Ph.D. in *What Causes
ADHD?*

The Myth of the A.D.D. Child, 1997. *50 Ways to Improve Your
Child's Behavior & Attention Span Without Drugs, Labels or
Coercion,* Thomas Armstrong PhD. An excellent introduction
describing the history of the use of psychiatric medications and some good
suggestions in terms of lifestyle changes .

Natural Prozac, 1988. Joel Robertson, Ph.D. Non-pharmaceutical
treatment solutions for depression and related disorders. Excellent
explanation of how chemical imbalances are related to depression and
their origins. Robertson also documents how music can influence
the chemistry of the mind and contribute to mental health disorders. Practical ideas for overcoming depression are found in this book.

No Child Left Different, 2006. Edited by Sharna Olfman, Ph.D.
Point Park University. Praeger Publishers: Childhood in
America series. http://www.pointpark.edu/def
Discusses issues, medications, child-rearing, ADHD, bipolar disorder,
and violence. Articles from a number of well-known writers, doctors
and experts in the field·

Please Don't Label My Child, 2007. Scott M. Shannon, M.D.
A balanced look at labeling children and the current psychiatric
method of labeling and medicating. A counter-viewpoint from the
mainstream approach, which makes much more sense. Shannon is a
pediatric psychiatrist who does prescribe medication at times.
Excellent chapter on labeling, other pertinent information.

Prozac Backlash (2000). Dr. Joseph Glennmullen, (psychiatrist). Provides some useful insight as to the limitations of psychiatric medications. Gives good suggestions with emphasis on addressing lifestyle changes rather than an over-reliance on pharmaceutical medications. See also The Antidepressant Solution.

Reading Recovery

International organization that gives assistance to schools in tutoring, reading for first-graders. www.readingrecovery.org

Remotely Controlled – How television is damaging our lives – and what we can do about it, (2005). Dr. Aric Sigman. How watching even moderate amounts of television can affect health and mental health, including depression in adults and children, as well as ADHD.

Rethinking ADHD, (1997). Ruth Schmidt Neven, Vicki Anderson, Tim Godber. Integrated approaches to helping children at home and at school. One of the best books on the subject. It discusses causes for ADHD, as well as documenting overmedication issue, social issues. Solution-oriented.

So Sexy, So Soon, (2007). Diane Levin, Ph.D. The media's and cultural influences on sexualizing children in modern society. Some of the media icons and influences mentioned by name in *So Sexy So Soon* are: Bratz Dolls, sexy cartoons, Pro-wrestling Girls, Power Puff Girls, Disney Channel, High School Musical, Spice Girls (Let Me Be Your Lover), Christina Agueleira, L'll Kim, 50-Cent, Justin Timberlake (Sexy Back), Eminem, Barbie Lingerie - My Scene Barbie, Cosmo Girl (magazine), sexy music videos, cable TV in the bedroom. One might add also, since the So Sexy So Soon book was published, Miley Cyrus' *Party in he USA* video and concert, with her controversial "pole dancing," as well as the Disney-produced Cheetah Girls. Lady Gaga is referred to by one news broadcast as "poison" for kids in a report entitled, "Has Lady Gaga Gone Too Far?," because of the strong sexual content of her video.

70% of TV for teens has sexual content. The average teen sees 2,000 sex acts a year on TV.

ICON VIOLENCE: Mighty Morphin Power Rangers, Transformers, Star Wars, Teenage Mutant Ninja Turtles, Pro-Wrestling, Grand Theft Auto (and others), GiJo.

Note: Handheld video game units pack a powerful punch. In grade school, playing hand-held video game units during recess, children kill-thy-neighbor in interactive combat and indulge in pocket sized criminal activity in Grand Theft Auto during class breaks. Does it affect their behavior in class? Does it affect their ability to concentrate, their academic performance and grades, their personality? It very likely does.

What Causes ADHD?, 2006. Joel T. Nigg, Ph.D. Michigan State University. Technical and thorough scientific insights into the subject, very well documented. Way beyond the scope of most books on ADHD. Very well-rounded in its scope. Again, a must for writers, authors on children's issues.

Your Child's Health, 1991. Barton D. Schmidt, M.D., F.A.A.P. Excellent general reference for parents and children's health. Chapters highlighting dangers of violence in TV and films for children. Barton documents the mental health implications for children of the past two decades, many of whom are indulging in movies of extreme violence and sadism from as young as kindergarten.

One other book of note for parents (and educators) is, **Mommy I'm Scared: How TV and Movies Frighten Children and What Parents Can Do About it,** by Joanne Cantor, Ph.D., professor of communication at University of Wisconsin.

Overall effects over time of media violence: Desensitization towards violence and to others' suffering imitation of violence/violent acts.   Children are often exposed to violence on the television at home, and parents mgiht not be aware of this. This is not uncommon and few use parents use parental   controls on TV or Internet. Cantor mentions by name, Jaws (movie) - The Day After, The Incredible Hulk, Batman, Goosebumps, E.T. (for young children), Alfred Hitchcock's Psycho, When a Stranger Calls (1979, 2006), the Wizard of Oz   (mentioned also by child psychiatrist Peter Neubeauer in the same context), as   examples of movies and TV with violence or disturbing scenes.   Also mentioned are the well known "Chucky," Friday the 13th and Freddy Krueger type movies, that children are regularly exposed to on cable TV and in the movie theatres.

Her book points to both problems and solutions. Part of that solution might be in education, where teachers, principals or other community educators can help parents to understand the value of protecting children from violence on television and in the media in general.

> A number of the books mentioned on these pages, of much social value, are available on googlebooks at no cost.

ADHD & Mental Health Checklist
for Parents and Educators

Art

If a child is visually oriented, what about enrolling your children in an art program or private lessons?

Have you looked into professional art therapy?

Do you have art books available at home for your child so he or she might develop their interest in art?

Can you spend some time teaching your children to enjoy art?

Diet

Does my child eat a good breakfast every day?

If my child has breakfast at school, do I know that he or she actually eats breakfast daily? What is he or she eating for breakfast at home or at school?

Can improvements be made in diet and nutrition?

Does my child consume a lot of sugar in different forms?

Does my child consume caffeine through soda or coffee/tea?

Green Therapy & Exercise

Have I included "green time" in my child's daily or weekly schedule? Parks, walking, hiking?

Does my child get exercise at least several times a week, at other times besides at school?

Environmental Contaminants

Is lead poisoning a possibility?
Other environmental contaminants?

Can I contact the local lead poisoning agency for testing if my home or apartment might be susceptible to lead or other environmental contamination?

Is my child very sensitive to additives in food?
If so, can adjustments be made in a balanced way for a more healthful diet?

Has my child or teen been experimenting with drugs or alcohol?

Education

Am I satisfied that my child is receiving the individualized attention he needs within the school system?

Do I take an active interest in his or her school work, sitting down and helping with homework after school?

Do I communicate regularly with his or her teachers?

Does the school have an after-school program to help with homework or reading?

Is there a program for free tutoring with the school or school district?

Does the local or county library have any special programs in tutoring or reading that can be of help?

Are there provisions within the school system for a personal assistant for my child?

Is there a special summer program or camp that my child could benefit from?

Are there academies within the school district where there may be fewer children in the classroom, or where the atmosphere might better facilitate my child's special needs?

Social, educational, spiritual and support

Have I made any efforts for him to have wholesome association with other children in the community, congregation, or school, or is he or she largely isolated?

Have I looked into music lessons for my child after school or on the weekends?

Have I looked into mentoring programs, especially if the child's father is absent?

How much time do I spend with my child giving him/her undivided attention?

If my child is a pre-teenager, do I spend time every day or night reading with him or her?

If the child has supportive grandparents, does he or she spend time with them regularly?

Have I instilled in my child a value system, and am I providing spiritual training?

Would a regular Bible study give a child needed support or some other form of mentoring?

What about seeking the assistance of a professional coach?

If my child needs the help of a psychologist or therapist, do I realize that medicine is an option, not a requirement?

Sexuality

In the case of a teenager or even some pre-teens, is he or she sexually active?

Might your teenager (or child) be dabbling in or be exposed to pornography on the Internet or television, with friends or elsewhere? [92]

Do you have parental control filtering software installed on your computer and/or on your child's cell phone, [93] if it has access to the Internet?

Discipline

Am I consistent?
Do I give discipline with firm but reasonable limits? Is the discipline administered with love?

Music

What music does my children or teen listen to? Is it intense or soft? How much time does he or she spend listening to music daily or weekly?

Electronics

How many hours of television does my child watch every day? How many hours of video games does my child play daily?

How many of hours of movies does my child view each week? What types of movies does he or she view? Are they calm, or are they aggressive or violent?

---

[92] Exposure to pornography can make it difficult for children to concentrate in school and can contribute to symptoms related to some mental health difficulties. Pornography exposure can be an issue for young children, as well as teens.

[93] There is software for parental internet control that can be installed on cell phones. Cell phones that have access to the Internet are a common mode of downloading and transmitting pornographic images for some children and teens.

Is my child being exposed to violence in the media? Cartoon violence? Action violence? Video game violence?

Has he developed a fondness for fantasy creatures, or violent fantasies? [94]

How many hours a day does my child spend on online social networking communities such as MySpace and in using the internet? Is he or she largely isolated from real social contacts after school?

What adjustments can be made?

If a child stays late in school daily, how is he using his time there? How does he use the computer system at school after hours?

Emotional and Support

If a child has deep-rooted emotional wounds from the present or past, has he or she opened up and talked to you or to a counselor?

Is there professional support for talk therapy available in school? [95]

Would you or your family benefit from family therapy, family counseling, or a support group?

---

[94] Suggestion from Dr. Armstrong's book, *The Myth of the A.D.D. Child - 50 Ways of to Improve Your Child's Behavior and Attention Span Without Drugs, Labels or Coercion.* A good reference book.

[95] Talk therapy, or Interpersonal Therapy, is sometimes especially helpful for children and teens.

75

Conclusion

In considering the subject of ADHD, much can be done to help children in the way of prevention, and to help them in overcoming symptoms associated with ADHD. In nearly all situations, prescription medication for ADHD can be avoided, and children can be helped in a balanced way, without having to resort to drugs. Many parents have found that drugs for ADHD are a temporary stop-gap at best, and have successfully worked with their children in different ways to help them to overcome their symptoms.

Childhood depression has similarly been successfully overcome through lifestyle changes. This information should be encouraging for parents, and give incentive for them to continue to work hard for the success of their children. Educators play a vital role in providing a healthy and creative classroom environment that is both stable and nurturing. This can do much to help marginal children to succeed as well.

Many parents need, themselves, to be educated and receive training on how to deal with difficult children and in child rearing. With this type of help, with the will to be successful, and by availing oneself of already available resources, and by putting forth effort into lifestyle changes, most children who display symptoms of ADHD can be helped by parents and educators, without medication, and succeed both at school and at home.

"Turn off the TV so that in reading you may better be."
Children of Paterson, NJ

Further Reading and Research

Further Reading and Research

1. The Art of Embracing ADHD
   by Daniella Barroqueira, Illinois State University

2. Art Helps ADHD
   Inspirational experience of grade and middle school teacher

3. Children's television impacts executive function and contributes to later attention problems, *University of Virginia*

4. *Time listening to popular music correlated with Major Depressive Disorder in adolescents, University of Pittsburgh*

5. Music and iPod school policies

6. ISU study finds TV viewing, video game play contribute to kids' attention problems, *Iowa State University*

7. ISU study proves conclusively that violent video game play makes more aggressive kids, *Iowa State University*

8. *Adjusting to Attention Deficit Disorder in adulthood, David Rabiner, Duke University*

9. ADHD/ADD and Depression, *David Rabiner, Duke University*

10. FDA Alert – Liver injury risk and market withdrawal

11. Bipolar disorder overdiagnosed by 50%

The Art of Embracing ADHD

By Dr. Daniella R. Barroqueiro
Associate Professor of Art Education, Illinois State University

When talking about ADHD, it is common to focus on the "downside" of the disorder, the challenges, the frustration, how to "fix" a problem or a set of problems. Notice I refer to a downside, which implies that there is also an upside to having ADHD. Intelligence, creativity, spontaneity and the ability to hyper-focus (yes, hyper-focus) are among the characteristics commonly found in people with ADHD.

Understandably, these assets are often framed in the negative because the person's ADHD is not working for them, but against them. Without a diagnosis, an awareness or knowledge of the disorder and the appropriate medications and/or behavior modifications, these assets are obscured by the numerous liabilities of the condition. For example:

Intelligence: "She is intelligent; her test scores are high, but she is not working to her potential. She is an underachiever."

Creativity: "He has a creative energy but never seems to complete anything, so he has little to show for it."

Spontaneity: "He is so spontaneous; he just flies by the seat of his pants. He doesn't seem to know how to plan ahead or follow a schedule."

Hyper-focus: "She is so obsessed with _____ that she doesn't get any of her work done. (Fill in the blank.)"

As an art educator with ADHD, I have been both a student with ADHD and a teacher of students with ADHD. I have heard some of these things said about me, and I have said some of these things about my students. In the public schools (and at the college level), the art room is often the one place where those with ADHD feel at home. Of course, there are many students who have little interest in art making, but I believe there is something to be learned from the art education model.

The inherent subjectivity of the discipline allows for more flexibility in the way lessons are taught and in the way students interpret assignments. Even in teacher-directed projects there is often room (or at least there should be) for the self-expression of each individual student. Many lessons are necessarily restrictive in the sense that they focus on teaching a particular technique or deal with a specific subject or theme, but even in these types of lessons there are usually opportunities for students with ADHD to attend to their particular interests or their idiosyncratic ways of working, which in turn helps them to stay focused on the task at hand. Strictly speaking, there is no one right or wrong way to paint or to sculpt something. (As I write these words I hear a list of contradictory thoughts disproving this statement, but this is an opinion piece and I am going to just go with it. I invite you to join me.)

The point is that when those with ADHD find (or create) an environment supportive to their needs, then ADHD becomes a non-issue, and in some cases, an asset. The trick is to figure out how to find or create that environment. It is my belief that when people with

ADHD have taken the time to learn about ADHD in general and their own "custom brand" of ADHD in particular, they have taken the first step. Once they have begun the process of minimizing their liabilities, harnessing their creative energy and finding a productive outlet for their intelligence and hyper-focus, the possibilities are endless. The potential for success and the enjoyment of life is enormous!

Remember there are two sides to every coin. It is one thing to accept you have ADHD, but it is another to embrace it. To those with ADHD, I recommend flipping the coin and embracing what you find on the other side. I'll bet it looks a lot like intelligence, creativity, spontaneity and the ability to focus on things that matter not only to you, but also to the rest of the world.

Reprinted with kind permission from Dr. Barroqueir

Art Helps ADHD
Inspirational Experience of Grade and Middle School Teacher

Ryan M. is an art teacher in one of the most difficult grade/middle schools in Newark, NJ. He has been teaching there for a number of years and has a good rapport with the students. He is difficult to frazzle, and students request to work in his class during their breaks. He rides his bike to work for exercise, and samples of his art work, along with the work of his students, aligns the walls of his classroom. He creates some striking landscapes in vibrant colors.

Mr. M. describes his personality growing up as antsy and hyperactive. He was diagnosed with ADHD as a young teen and prescribed Ritalin, then Adderall from middle school years through high school. However, he did not like to take the medication because of the strong side effects. He didn't like the way it made him feel, and he felt that the medication contributed to a rage inside of him that was difficult to deal with.

When he graduated high school, he took up art in college, something he always enjoyed doing. He stopped taking the stimulant medications, graduated college and became an art teacher. He continues to work on his own art projects after school, but has no noticeable issues with hyperactivity or inattention. He is well-adjusted and an asset to the school, contributing to the success and development of the children he works with.

He said that there were only two things that helped him with his ADHD symptoms during his school years, playing soccer and art. He doesn't play so much soccer now, but he continues to work with art. His experience is so similar to that of Professor Barroqueiro, that it is worth mentioning here and may be an encouragement for some parents to consider directing their children towards art if they are struggling with attentional problems or hyperactivity.

Art Helps ADHD *article with permission and approval from Ryan M.*

Children's Television [aka - Sponge Bob] Impacts Children's Executive Function and Contributes to Later Attention Problems

In a study entitled, **The Immediate Impact of Different Types of Television on Young Children's Executive Function by professor** Angeline S. Lillard, PhD, and Jennifer Peterson, BA of the *Department of Psychology at the University of Virginia, Charlottesville, Virginia, researchers concluded that children's television can have a marked affect on attention problems. The paper, published September 12, 2011 in Pediatrics, states that "Previous study results have suggested a longitudinal association between entertainment television and later attention problems."*

What this study adds is, *"Using a controlled experimental design, this study found that preschool aged children were significantly impaired in executive function immediately after watching just 9 minutes of a popular fast-paced television show [Sponge Bob] relative to after watching educational television or drawing."*

This study concludes what most of us could discern intuitively, that Sponge Bob, and other fast-paced cartoons, does indeed wind up the spring of children and can affect the attention and ability to concentrate in young children. In this study, sixty four-year-old preschool children were assigned to watch a fastpaced television cartoon, a realistic educational cartoon or to draw for nine minutes.

The children who were assigned to watch the educational cartoon and the children who were assigned to draw, performed significantly better in executive function tasks than those who watched the fastpaced cartoon.

The study states that "Parents should be aware that fast-paced television shows could at least temporarily impair young children's executive function."

Functions associated with the Executive Function (EF) are part of the skills associated with the prefrontal cortex, which include, goal-directed behavior, attention, working memory, inhibitory control, problem solving, self-regulation and delay of gratification (as opposed to instant gratification, commonly associated with television). EF is recognized as a key to "positive social and cognitive functioning." Therefore, EF has a bearing on the overall success of children in school, on a wide range of fronts. Long-term effects of watching television for children have been documented in some studies, this was the first to consider short-term effects. The study states that "even adults report feeling less alert immediately after watching television." And that "Entertainment television is particularly associated
with long-term attention problems."

Sesame Street upped the pace of television for children, starting around 1968/1969, however, Sesame Street today is double the pace of Sesame Street when it began over 30 years ago, states Lillard and Paterson.

In addition to the fast pace of the cartoon, the authors hypothesize that the "onslaught of fantastical events," portrayed in the cartoon shown to the children in this study, may have further exacerbated the Executive Function of the children. Additionally, the study does not make conclusions about the long-term effects of watching fastpaced television, and because the cartoon segments were only nine minutes, compared to longer period of time typically involved with television cartoons for children, the actual effects on EF, including attention, may actually be "more detrimental" than the study indicates.

The authors state that "Children watch a great deal of television," which "has been associated with long-term," and in the case of this study "short-term" attentional problems.

Further information on Executive Function:

Kaplan S, Berman M. Directed attention as a common resource for executive functioning and self-regulation. *Perspectives Psychol Sci.* 2010;5(1):43

The Immediate Impact of Different Types of Television on Young Children's Executive Function
Angeline S. Lillard and Jennifer Peterson
Pediatrics; originally published online September 12, 2011;
DOI: 10.1542/peds.2010-1919
http://pediatrics.aappublications.org/content/early/2011/09/08/peds.2010-1919.full.pdf

Time Listening to Popular Music Correlated with Major Depressive Disorder in Adolescents

Researchers at the University of Pittsburgh concluded that there is a correlation between Major Depression and the amount of time an adolescent spends with popular music. Conversely, Major Depression is negatively, or reversely correlated with reading print media such as books. The study, published in the Archives of Pediatric and Adolescent Medicine, April, 2011, examined data collected through telephone interviews. During an eight-week period involving one-hundred six adolescents. The study was part of a larger neurobehavioral study of depression that was conducted between 2003 and 2008.

For each increasing quartile of audio/music use, there was an 80% increase in the odds of having Major Depression (MDD). For time spent reading, there was a 50% decrease in the odds of having MDD.

The study does not necessarily conclude a direct cause and effect relationship, although that might be one valid conclusion. Rather, there might be other correlational factors to consider in evaluating this evidence. Perhaps those who are more inclined towards music are also more inclined towards major depression. Perhaps those with major depression seek solace and solitude in music.

In any case, there seems to be strong evidence that for adolescents, there is a correlation between time spent listening to popular music and depression. This can provide encouragement for parents, educators and mental health professionals to help children and adolescents spend less time listening to popular music and more time reading.

Reference:
Using Ecological Momentary Assessment to Determine Media Use by Individuals With and Without Major Depressive Disorder. Brian A. Primack, MD, EdM, MS; Jennifer S. Silk, PhD; Christian R. DeLozier, BS; William G. Shadel, PhD; Francesca R. Dillman Carpentier, PhD; Ronald E. Dahl, MD;Galen E. Switzer, PhD. *Arch Pediatr Adolesc Med.* 2011;165(4):360-365. doi:10.1001/archpediatrics.2011.27
http://archpedi.ama-assn.org/cgi/content/abstract/165/4/360

Music and iPod School Policies

Many schools have a difficult time keeping the use of electronic devices in school and in the classroom under control. One vice-principal in a city grammar and middle school declared that the administration was waging a "war on electronic devices" in school, similar to the "war on drugs" from a previous decade. She said that "we know that we won't completely win this war, but we'll keep trying."

In the International Grammar School in Sydney, Australia, the administration outright banned iPods, "the gadget of choice" in school. (An iPod can hold up to 10,000 songs, although most students might have only one or two-hundred at any one time). Not all students concurred, stating that listening to music while doing school work helped them to concentrate, however, the school administration disagreed referring to iPods and similar devices as contributing to "social isolation," The executive director of the Association of Independent Schools, Geoff Newcombe stated that iPods in school "distract students, impede their safety and stop them from communicating with classmates."

Many teachers, however, downplay the issue and allow students to listen to iPods in class, especially if students are quiet and do their work.

One of the problems, though, with electronics in school is, as one Newark High School Graphic Arts teacher stated, "give them an inch and they take a mile". It can be very difficult to keep electronic devices under control once they are in the school and when there may be inconsistent or loosely enforced guidelines. Both teachers and administration get worn out with the issue, and as the school year progresses use of electronics gets out of hand. This situation can contribute to a lower quality in the academic level of individual schools.

In Barringer Preparatory High School in Newark, New Jersey, iPods and other electronic devices are banned in school. Not an iPod (or their equivalents) can be seen in the hallways and students attempting to bring them in, get stopped at the metal detectors and are required to turn in their electronics at the door before coming in the school hallway. They can then collect their devices at the end of the day, a rather humane anecdote to a problem that perplexes some school systems. Students seem no worse for the wear, in fact, it is a school, in a very difficult area of Newark to teach in, where there is good order in the hallways, and where security guards are able to keep on top of both the hallways and security issues in the classrooms without getting into needless confrontations with students.

Reference: No more songs in their pockets: School bans iPods. By Linda Doherty and Jordan Baker. *The Sydney Morning Herald.*

ISU study finds TV viewing, video game play contribute to kids' attention problems

AMES, Iowa - Parents looking to get their kid's attention - or keeping them focused at home and in the classroom - should try to limit their television viewing and video game play. That's because a new study led by three Iowa State University psychologists has found that both viewing television and playing video games are associated with increased attention problems in youths.

The research, which included both elementary school-age and college-age participants, found that children who exceeded the two hours per day of screen time recommended by the American Academy of Pediatrics were 1.5 to 2 times more likely to be above average in attention problems.

"There isn't an exact number of hours when screen time contributes to attention problems, but the AAP recommendation of no more than two hours a day provides a good reference point," said Edward Swing, an Iowa State psychology doctoral candidate and lead researcher in the study. "Most children are way above that. In our sample, children's total average time with television and video games is 4.26 hours per day, which is actually low compared to the national average."

Collaborating with Swing on the research were ISU's Douglas Gentile, an associate professor of psychology and Craig Anderson, a Distinguished Professor of psychology; and David Walsh, a Minneapolis psychologist. Their study will be published in the August print issue of Pediatrics -- the journal of the American Academy of Pediatrics.

Studies on elementary, college-aged youths

The researchers assessed 1,323 children in third, fourth and fifth grades over 13 months, using reports from the parents and children about their video game and television habits, as well as teacher reports of attention problems. Another group of 210 college students provided self-reports of television habits, video game exposure and attention problems.

Previous research had associated television viewing with attention problems in children. The new study also found similar effects from the amount of time spent with video games.

"It is still not clear why screen media may increase attention problems, but many researchers speculate that it may be due to rapid-pacing, or the natural attention grabbing aspects that television and video games use," Swing said.
Gentile reports that the pace of television programming has been quickened by "the MTV effect.

"When MTV came on, it started showing music videos that had very quick edits -- cuts once every second or two," Gentile said. "Consequently, the pacing of other television and films sped up too, with much quicker edits."

He says that quicker pace may have some brain-changing effects when it comes to attention span. "Brain science demonstrates that the brain becomes what the brain does," Gentile said. "If we train the brain to require constant stimulation and constant flickering lights, changes in sound and camera angle, or immediate feedback, such as video games can provide, then when the child lands in the classroom where the teacher doesn't have a million-dollar-per-episode budget, it may be hard to get children to sustain their attention." The study showed that the effect was similar in magnitude between video games and TV viewing.

TV, video games may contribute to ADHD

Based on the study's findings, Swing and Gentile conclude that TV and video game viewing may be one contributing factor for attention deficit hyperactivity disorder (ADHD) in children.

"ADHD is a medical condition, but it's a brain condition," Gentile said. "We know that the brain adapts and changes based on the environmental stimuli to which it is exposed repeatedly. Therefore, it is not unreasonable to believe that environmental stimuli can increase the risk for a medical condition like ADHD in the same way that environmental stimuli, like cigarettes, can increase the risk for cancer."

"Although we did not specifically study the medical condition of ADHD in these studies, we did focus on the kinds of attention problems that are experienced by students with ADHD," added Swing. "We were surprised, for example, that attention problems in the classroom would increase in just one year for those children with the highest screen time."

Author of study: Craig Anderson, Psychology, Iowa State University
Articles on this and following page reprinted with permission from Iowa State University News Service
http://www.news.iastate.edu/news/2010/jul/TVVGattention

ISU study proves conclusively that violent video game play makes more aggressive kids

AMES, Iowa -- Iowa State University Distinguished Professor of Psychology Craig Anderson has made much of his life's work studying how violent video game play affects youth behavior. And he says a new study he led, analyzing 130 research reports on more than 130,000 subjects worldwide, proves conclusively that exposure to violent video games makes more aggressive, less caring kids -- regardless of their age, sex or culture.

The study was published today in the March 2010 issue of the Psychological Bulletin, an American Psychological Association journal. It reports that exposure to violent video games is a causal risk factor for increased aggressive thoughts and behavior, and decreased empathy and prosocial behavior in youths.

"We can now say with utmost confidence that regardless of research method -- that is experimental, correlational, or longitudinal -- and regardless of the cultures tested in this study [East and West], you get the same effects," said Anderson, who is also director of Iowa State's Center for the Study of Violence. "And the effects are that exposure to violent video games increases the likelihood of aggressive behavior in both short-term and long-term contexts. Such exposure also increases aggressive thinking and aggressive affect, and decreases prosocial behavior."

The study was conducted by a team of eight researchers, including ISU psychology graduate students Edward Swing and Muniba Saleem; and Brad Bushman, a former Iowa State psychology professor who now is on the faculty at the University of Michigan. Also on the team were the top video game researchers from Japan - Akiko Shibuya from Keio University and Nobuko Ihori from Ochanomizu University - and Hannah Rothstein, a noted scholar on meta-analytic review from the City University of New York.

Reprinted with permission from Iowa State University News Service
http://www.news.iastate.edu/news/2010/mar/vvgeffects

Reprinted with permission from David Rabiner, Ph.D., Director of Undergraduate Studies. Dept. of Psychology & Neuroscience. Senior Research Scientist. Center for Child and Family Policy

Adjusting to Attention Deficit Disorder in adulthood

On the positive side, approximately one third of children with ADHD/ADD appear to be relatively well adjusted and symptom free as young adults. Although reliable predictors of such good adult outcome have not been fully identified there are several factors that are important to note.

First, not surprisingly, higher levels of intellectual functioning and better school performance are associated with better outcomes. Second, the absence of severe behavior and conduct problems during childhood, particularly before age 10, is associated with better adult outcome. And finally, children with ADHD/ADD who manage to get along well with their peers are likely to have better adjustments as adults.

These factors have clear implications for parents. It is very important to stress that it does not appear to be the primary symptoms of ADHD/ADD - inattention, hyperactivity, and impulsivity - that are most directly responsible for the negative adult outcomes that many children with ADHD/ADD attain. Instead, it is the behavioral, social, and academic difficulties that children with ADHD/ADD are at increased risk for that may be most clearly linked to negative adult outcome.

What this means is that if parents can succeed in preventing the development of these secondary problems - i.e. academic struggles, social problems, severe behavioral problems - their child is likely to have a much more successful adjustment in adolescence and young adulthood. Carefully monitoring a child's overall development, and not just focusing on ADHD/ADD symptoms, is thus critically important. When academic, behavioral, and social difficulties arise, working hard to address these problems is of paramount importance.

The following is quoted from *Medication Treatment for ADHD*, David Rabiner, Ph.D., Duke University

* What other interventions have already been tried?
Some children with ADHD can have their symptoms effectively managed via other means including appropriate behavioral and educational interventions. If you are concerned about using medication with your child, make sure that non-medical interventions have been tried first. This is an important issue to discuss with your child's physician. It is important to be aware, however, that no form of treatment has been shown to be as effective as stimulant medication for the majority of children with ADHD.

* How much difficulty are my child's symptoms actually creating?
The degree of impairment in academic, social, and behavioral functioning caused by ADHD can vary substantially. If the impairment experienced by your child is on the modest side, medication can be less essential than when the impairment is great.

* What is my child's attitude towards taking medication?
It is very important to discuss the rational for using medication with the child. The child needs to know why it is being suggested and how it can be helpful. This is especially

true for older children and adolescents, who may have concerns about being teased should their peers find out that they are taking medicine. If children have strong objections to taking medication, these should be discussed and understood. Should these objections persist, using medication may not be productive.

* Will objective information about the effects of medication be provided?
In my opinion, this is critical. Despite the well documented benefits of stimulant medication, as many as 20-30% of children do not experience significant benefits. In addition, many parents are surprised to learn that when children with ADHD receive only a placebo (i.e. medication that appears to be the real thing but is not), teachers frequently report significant improvement in the child's behavior. This means that some children may receive stimulant medication for a sustained period even though they derive no objective benefit from it.

What causes this placebo effect? No one knows for sure, but when teachers are aware that a child has started medication, it is difficult for them to provide an objective, unbiased account of the child's behavior. Some children may also do better when they believe they are receiving medication that is supposed to help. This can make it difficult for parents and physicians to get objective information to use in making decisions about long term medication use.

*****

Despite the placebo effect noted above, there are many children for whom the response is so dramatic that it seems impossible to attribute the improvement to a simple placebo response. Studies have found, however, that sometimes the improvement reported when a child is receiving placebo can also be quite dramatic. In addition, determining the optimum dose for a child in the absence of receiving objective feedback is also difficult.

End quote - Dr. Rabiner then describes a method by which parents, along with teachers, can test whether or not medication is actually affecting a positive response or if there are other factors that are mainly responsible.

See: Medication Treatment for ADHD, David Rabiner, Ph.D.
Help for ADHD newsletter. http://www.helpforadd.com/medical-treatment/

ADHD/ADD and Depression

Several well conducted have shown that children with Attention Deficit Hyperactivity Disorder/Attention Deficit Disorder are more likely than others to become depressed at some time during their development. In fact, their risk for developing depression is as much as 3 times greater than for other children.

What does depression look like in a child?

What, then, would a "typical" depressed child look like? Although there of course would be wide variations from child to child, such a child might seem to be extremely irritable and/or very sad, and this would represent a distinct change from their typical state. They might stop participating or getting excited about things they used to enjoy and display a distinct change in eating patterns. You would notice them as being less energetic, they might complain about being unable to sleep well, and they might start referring to themselves in critical and disparaging ways. It is also quite common for school grades to suffer as their concentration is impaired, as does their energy to devoted to any task. As noted above, this pattern of behavior would persist for at least several weeks, and would appear as a real change in how the child typically is. (It is also important to note, however, that some children can experience a chronic, somewhat less intense type of mood disorder that is called dysthymic disorder. In this disorder, there is a pervasive and ongoing pattern of depressed mood rather than a more distinct change from the child's typical way of appearing).

Depression and Children with Attention Deficit Hyperactivity Disorder/Attention Deficit Disorder

As noted above, children with ADHD/ADD appear to be at increased risk for the development of depression. In addition, it is important to recognize that in some children, the symptoms of depression can be incorrectly diagnosed as reflecting ADHD/ADD. That is because diminished concentration, failing to complete tasks, and even agitated behavior that can resemble hyperactive symptoms can often be found in children who are depressed. It is thus quite important to be certain that depression has been ruled out as an explanation for the symptoms of ADHD/ADD a child may be displaying. Having said this, please remember that for many children, Attention Deficit Hyperactivity Disorder/Attention Deficit Disorder and depression can co-occur - i.e. be present at the same time. Thus, it is not always a matter of ruling out depression to diagnose ADHD/ADD, or ruling out ADHD/ADD and diagnosing depression. This is because in some situations both diagnoses would be appropriate and is one of the reasons why a careful evaluation by a trained child mental health professional can be so important to have done.

Recent research has suggested that in children with ADHD/ADD who are depressed, the depression is not simply the result of demoralization that can result from the day to day struggles that having ADHD/ADD can cause. Instead, although such struggles may be an important risk factor that makes the development of depression in children with Attention Deficit Hyperactivity Disorder/Attention Deficit Disorder more likely, depression in children with ADHD/ADD is often a distinct disorder and not merely "demoralization". The results of one recent study indicated that the strongest predictor of persistent major depression in children with ADHD/ADD was interpersonal difficulties (i.e. being unable to get along well with peers). In contrast, school difficulty and severity of Attention Deficit Hyperactivity Disorder/Attention Deficit Disorder symptoms were not associated with persistent major depression. In addition, the marked diminishment of ADHD/ADD symptoms did not necessarily predict a corresponding remission of depressive symptoms. In other words, the course of ADHD/ADD symptoms and the course of depressive symptoms in this sample of children appeared to be relatively distinct.

Implications

Depression in children can be effectively treated with psychological intervention. In fact, the evidence to support the efficacy of psychological interventions for depression in children and adolescents is currently more compelling than the evidence supporting the use of medication.

The important point that can be taken from this study, I think, is that parents need to be sensitive to recognizing the symptoms of depression in their child, and not to simply assume that it is just another facet of their child's ADHD/ADD. In addition, if a child with ADHD/ADD does develop depression as well, treatments that target the depressive symptoms specifically need to be implemented. As this study shows, one should not assume that just addressing the difficulties caused by the Attention Deficit Hyperactivity Disorder/Attention Deficit Disorder symptoms will also alleviate a child's depression. If you have concerns about depression in your child, a thorough evaluation by an experienced child mental health professional is strongly recommended. This can be a difficult diagnosis to correctly make in children, and you really want to be dealing with someone who has extensive experience in this area.

Article, ADHD/ADD and Depression reprinted with permission from David Rabiner, Ph.D. http://www.helpforadd.com/depression-with-add/

David Rabiner, Ph.D.
Director of Undergraduate Studies
Dept. of Psychology & Neuroscience
Senior Research Scientist
Center for Child and Family Policy
Duke University

FDA ALERT [10/2005]: Liver Injury Risk and Market Withdrawal.

The Federal Drug Administration has concluded that the overall liver toxicity from Cylert and generic pemoline products outweighs the benefits of this drug. In May 2005, Abbott chose to stop sales and marketing of Cylert in the U.S. All generic companies have also agreed to stop sales and marketing of this product in the U.S. (pemoline tablets and chewable tablets). Cylert is a central nervous system stimulant indicated for the treatment of Attention Deficit Hyperactivity Disorder (ADHD). This product is considered second-line therapy for ADHD, because of its association with life-threatening hepatic failure (see BOX WARNING in product label and patient package insert).

Bipolar Disorder Over-diagnosed by 50%

Using a self-administered questionnaire, Structured Clinical Interview for DSM-IV (SCID) and a review of the family history, the research team found that "fewer than half" of the patients diagnosed with bipolar disorder, actually met the criteria for this condition, based on the SCID diagnostic questionnaire. (Dr. Zimmerman at Brown Medical School).

In July 2009 a study of 82 patients previously (erroneously) diagnosed with bipolar disorder revealed that the vast majority - 68 of the 82 (82.9%) - had major depression. The majority of the others had eating disorders, anxiety disorders, borderline personality disorder, impulse control disorders, and other disorders, rather than bipolar disorder, according to the DSM-IV (SCID) test. Bipolar disorder "is typically treated with mood-stabilizing drugs that can have side effects -- including effects on the kidneys, liver, and metabolic and immune systems, and means some patients are likely not getting the appropriate care for the problems they do have."

"The results of this study suggest that bipolar disorder is being over-diagnosed," Zimmerman says. Such instances are cause for significant concern given the serious side effects of mood stabilizing drugs - the standard treatment for bipolar disorder, which include possible impact to renal, endocrine, hepatic, immunologic, and metabolic function. Patients and physicians are both susceptible to the misdiagnosis. Some patients "are looking for a magic pill that will cure all ills," Zimmerman told the Providence Journal, as a way to skirt the difficult work of psychotheraphy.

http://biomed.brown.edu/facultyupdate/news.php
http://www.winmentalhealth.com/bipolar.disorder.overdiagnosed.php

Charts and Graphs

Charts and Graphs

1. Psychotropic medication spending and use increase - 1993 to 2003.

2. Percentage of children watching R-rated and violent movies.

3. Possible contributing influences to ADHD.

4. Social regression and TV time.

5. Mental health dynamics.

Chart 1

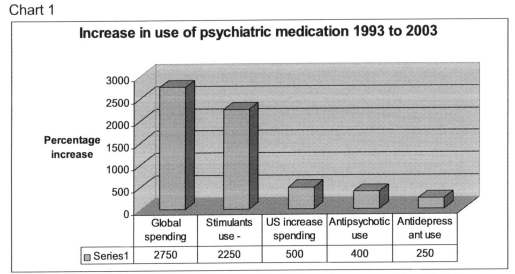

	Global spending	Stimulants use -	US increase spending	Antipsychotic use	Antidepress ant use
▣ Series1	2750	2250	500	400	250

Increase in stimulant use is for Australia/Britain. Chart is based on research from Ruth Neven, Ph.D., et al., from the book Rethinking ADHD, and from other sources.

Chart 2

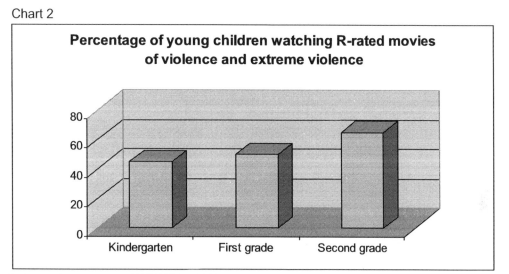

Percentage of young children watching R-rated movies of violence and extreme violence

Independent survey, (AYCNP), 2006 – 2007 of 70 public school children.
See Your Children's Health by Barton Schmidt, M.D., F.A.A.P., about health and mental/emotional dangers of children watching violent R-rated movies.

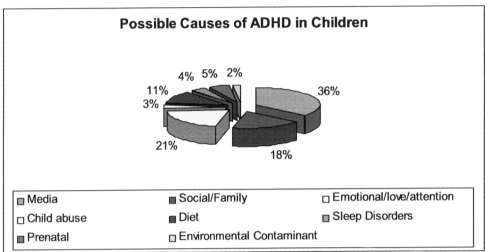

Possible Causes of ADHD in Children

4% 5% 2%
11%
3%
36%
21%
18%

☐ Media ☐ Social/Family ☐ Emotional/love/attention
☐ Child abuse ☐ Diet ☐ Sleep Disorders
☐ Prenatal ☐ Environmental Contaminant

Chart 3

This is a suggested list of possible causes or contributing influences for ADHD in children, and to a certain extent adults. Joel Nigg, Ph.D., in his book What Causes ADHD? Provides evidence that there are causes for the disorder. It is not something that arises unbidden, and that while there is a genetic predisposition for ADHD, it is the combination of genetic predisposition with a multitude of other factors that leads to the actual disorder.

The percentages offered in this graph are intuitive rather than scientific, and are meant to be applicable over a broad population and not for individuals. Some of the categories overlap such as Social/Family and Emotional/love/attention, child abuse. It must be remembered also, that any gaps in family life can contribute to other factors, even prenatal, in that, if a person's life is not in good order to begin with, then there is a greater chance that prenatal care might not be adequate, or that a child will not receive the love and attention he needs.

Poverty might also put one at greater risk for environmental contaminants such as lead poisoning. A larger percentage of old tenements may still have lead paint on the walls an paint chips that children might ingest. So, many of the factors in this list may be co-dependent or mutually influenced.

98

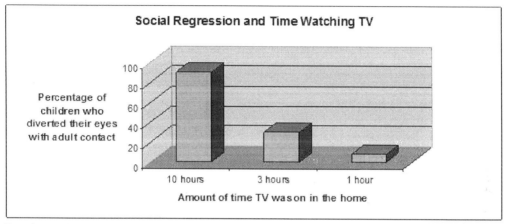

Based on study from the Japanese Pediatric Association   Chart 4

The Japanese Pediatric Association urges parents and doctors to keep children, especially those aged less than two, away from the television as much as possible after research findings showed that watching too much television impaired children's ability to develop personal relationships.

Daily Yomiuri online
http://www.yomiuri.co.jp/main//main-e.htm

Medical News Today
http://www.medicalnewstoday.com/articles/5799.php

Please see webpage for larger, readable version of Mental Health Dynamics chart.

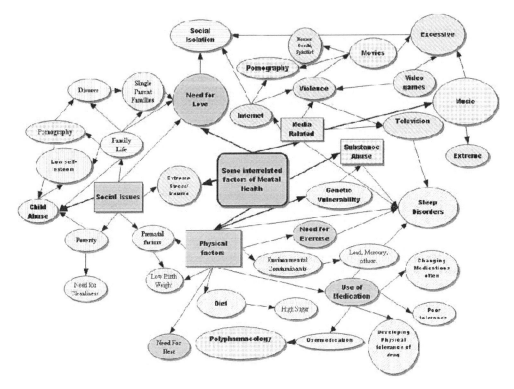

www.winmentalhealth.com/images/charts/mentalhealthchart.jpg

George Albee felt that social issues were at the root of mental health disorder for a significant percentage of the population. Urie Bronfenbrenner's Bioecological Model Urie Bronfenbrenner's Bioecological Model Provided for multiple factors, micro and macro, which contribute to mental health disorders. The mental health chart above is loosely configured around that model. Bronfenbrenner's Model for mental health is an infinitely more useful and accurate model as a foundation for insightl and as a foundation on which to build for all arease of mental health than the Medical Model, which has gradually come into vogue since the late 1950s, and in terms of ADHD, especially since the 1970s.

Bibliography

The ADDA Subcommittee on ADHD Coaching, (2002, November). *The ADHD Guiding Principles for Coaching Individuals with Attention Deficit Disorder.* Attention Deficit Disorder Association (ADDA). From ADDA database: www.add.org/articles /coachingguide.html

ADHD & Coexisting Conditions: Tics and Tourette Syndrome, (2005). *National Resource Center on AD/HD.* From CHADD website: http://www.help4adhd.org/documents/W WK5a1.pdf

ADHD in Children, (2010). Mayo Clinic http://www.mayoclinic.com/health/adhd/DS00275

Adult ADHD, (2010). Mayo Clinic http://www.mayoclinic.com/health/adult-adhd/DS01161

Armstrong, Thomas, (1997). *The Myth of the A.D.D. Child - 50 Ways to Improve Your Child's Behavior & Attention Span Without Drugs, Labels or Coercion.* New York: Penguin-Putman.

Ashley, S. Ph.D., (2005). *ADD & ADHD Answer Book-The Top 275 Questions Parents Ask.* Naperville, Il: Sourcebooks, Inc.

Attention-Deficit / Hyperactivity Disorder (ADHD), 2010. Center for Disease Prevention and Control (CDC). http://www.cdc.gov/ncbddd/adhd/diagnosis.html

Barkley, R., Ph.D., (1997). *ADHD and the Nature of Self Control.* New York: Guildford.

Barkley, R., Murphy, K. R., Fischer, M., (2008). ADHD in Adults: What the Science Says. New York: Guildford.

Barkley, R., (1995). *Taking Charge of ADHD: The Complete, Authoritative Guide for Parents.* New York: Guilford.

Barroqueiro, D. Ed.D., (2006). The Art of Embracing AD/HD. *Attention Deficit Disorder Association (ADDA).* http://www.add.org/e-newsletters/May07.htm

Barrow, K., (2006, July 6). *The Ritalin Generation Goes to College.* About.com newsletter.

Bee, H., Boyd., D., (2007). *The Developing Child, 11th Edition.* Boston: Pearson p. 66

Behavior & Development: the Trouble with TV. Too much television can have a negative effect on your child's math and reading scores. (2005, November) *Parents magazine* www.parents com/parents/story jsp

Beyond pills: 5 conditions you can improve with lifestyle changes. Harvard Health Newsletter www.health.harvard.edu

Bibliotherapy: Reading Your Way to Mental Health.(July 31, 2007). *The Wall Street Journal.* Pg. D1.

Bruhn, K., Waltz, S., Stephani, U., (2007, March). Screen sensitivity in photosensitivity children and adolescents: patient dependent and stimulus dependent factors. *PubMed.* From the National Library of Medicine database. www.pubmed.gov

Carey, B., (2007, May 3). FDA Expands Suicide Warnings on Drugs. *The New York Times.*

Case, Caroline & Dalley, (2008) . *Art Therapy with Children: From Infancy to Adolescence.* London: Karnac.

Center for Screentime Awareness. www.screetime.org

Christakis, D., Zimmerman, F DiGiussepe, D., (April 4, 2004). Early Television Exposure and Subsequent Attentional Problems in Children. *Pediatrics.* Vol. 113. No. 4. www.seattlechildrens .org

Cummings, H., (2007). Gamers Spend Less Time on Homework - Study Examines Video Games Among Adolescents. *Archives of Pediatrics and Adolescent Medicine. American Academy of Pediatrics.*

Don't let your baby watch too much TV says Japanese experts. *Daily Yomiuri Online.* www.yomiuri.com.jp.
www.medicalnewstoday.com /articles/5799.php.

Drug Withdrawal, (2004, December 20). *Time magazine.*
http://www.time.com/time/magazine/article/0,9171,1009789,00.html

Eide, Brock; Fernette Eide, (2006). *The Mislabeled Child.* New York: Hyperion

Edwards, E., (1989). *Drawing on the Right Side of the Brain.* New York: Tarcher/Putnam.

Exercise Can Reduce Depression. (January 8, 2002). *Watching the World, Awake!* New York.

Fahriye Oflaz PhD, Sevgi Hatipolu PhD, Hamdullah Aydin MD, (March 2008) Effectiveness of psychoeducation intervention on post-traumatic stress disorder and coping styles of earthquake survivors. *Journal of Clinical Nursing*, Vol 17, Issue 5, p. 677.687.

Fartery, E., (2000, October 4). Attention Deficit Disorder and a Mom's Heartaches. Clifton, NJ: *The Record.*
www.web2.bccls.org/web2/tram p2.exe/see_record.

FDA, (2005, September 30). FDA Issues Public health Advisory on Strattera (Atmoxetine) for Attention Deficit Disorder. *U.S. Food and Drug Administration.* Retrieved from FDA News database:
www.fda.gov/bbs /topics/NEW S/2005/NEW 01237.html

FDA Alert: Liver Injury Risk and Market Withdrawal, (2005, October). Alert for Healthcare Professionals: Pemoline Tablets and Chewable Tables (marketed as Cylert). *US Food and Drug Administration, Center for Drug Evaluation and Research.* http://www.fda.gov/downloads/Drugs/DrugSafety/PostmarketDrugSafetyl InformationforPatientsandProviders /ucm126462.pdf

FDA, (2005, September). Safety Alerts for Drugs, Biologics, Medical Devices, and Dietary Supplements. *FDA News.* Food and Drug Administration.

Gardener, A., (July 19, 2005). Ritalin and Cancer. HealthDay Reporter. http://www.playattention.com/attention-deficit/articles/ritalin-and-cancer/

Glenmullen, J., (2005). *The Antidepressant Solution.* New York: Free Press.

Glenmullen, J., (2000). Prozac *Backlash.* New York: Simon & Schuster.

Goode, Erica., (2003, January 14). Study finds jump in children taking psychiatric drugs *The New York Times*

Göpfert, M., Webster, J., Seeman, M.V., Professor Emerita Department of Psychiatry University of Toronto, (2004). Parental psychiatric disorder: distressed parents and their families.

Gottesman, R., Ed., (1999). *Violence in America.* New York: Charles Scribner, Sons.

Green, L, Ottoson, J., (1990). *Community and Population Health, Eighth Edition.* McGraw Hill.

Hallowell, E., M.D., Ratey, J. M.D., (1994). *Driven to Distraction Recognizing and Coping with Attention Deficit Disorder from Childhood Through Adulthood·* New York: Touchstone

Harris, G., (2006, November 23). Proof is Scant on Psychiatric Drug Mix for Young

Hill, K., Ed.D., (2005). *Personal Correspondence.* Paterson, NJ.

Holden, C., (2004, October 26). Prozac may actually raise anxiety levels in newborn mice. *Science Now.*

Huxsahl, John, E., M.D., (2010). Do Food Additives Cause ADHD? Mayo Clinic. http://www.mayoclinic.com/health/adhd/AN01721

Iannelli, V., (2006, July). ADHD in the Summer. ADHD newsletter, *About.com* http://pediatrics.about.com /od/adhd/a/06_adhd_summer.htm

Imam, S., M.D., MPH; Sargenet, J. M.D., (October 2, 2006). Association Between Television, Movie, and Video Game Exposure and School Performance. *Pediatrics.* http://pediatrics.aapublications.org/cgi/content/full/118/4/e1061

It's Easier Seeing Green - ADHD curbed when kids play outdoors. (2004, March/April). *Psychology Today.* p. 26,27.

Kelly, R, (2005, August 8). How to Quit the Cure-SSRIs. *Newsweek.*

King, S., Waschbusch, D., Pelham W., Jr, Frankland, B. W., Andrade, B. F., Jacques, S., Corkum, P. V., (December 24, 2008). Social Information Processing in Elementary-School Aged Children with ADHD: Medication Effects and Comparisons with Typical Children. *Journal of Abnormal Child Psychology.* http://www.springerlink .com/content/pp7675p0777qxj15/

King W. Babies, Toddlers watch lots of TV, new study finds. Seattle, WA: *Seattle Times.* www.seatletimes.nwsource.com .

Kluger, J., 2003, November 3). Are We Giving Our Kids Too Many Drugs? *Time Magazine.*

Kuo, F., E., Taylor, A. F., (2004). A Potential Natural Treatment for Attention-Deficit/Hyperactivity Disorder: Evidence From a National Study. *American Journal of Public Health.* http://ajph.aphapublications.org/cgi/content/abstract/94/9/1580

Kris L. L. Movig, PhD; Michiel W. H. E. Janssen, MD; Jan de Waal Malefijt, MD, PhD; Peter J. Kabel, MD, PhD; Hubert G. M. Leufkens, PhD; Antoine C. G. Egberts, PhD, (October 27, 2003). Relationship of Serotonergic Antidepressants and Need for Blood Transfusion in Orthopedic Surgical Patients. *Arch Intern Med, 203;* 163:2354-2358. http://archinte.am a-assn.org/cgi/content/full/163/

Lipkin, P., Butz, Cozen, (2003). High Dose Methylphenidate treatment of ADHD in a Preschooler. *PubMed.* From NCBI database: www.ncbi.nlm.nih.gov/pubmed/12804131?dopt=Abs tract.

Living With ADD. Tips to help live with ADD. *Living with ADD.* Plymouth, MD. www.livingwithADD.com/tips.html

Lugara, J., (2004, Oc tober). Disconnected from the real world: Is the new age of media & technology killing our kid's childhoods? New York : *Metro Parent Guide.*

Marsa, L., (2005, January 5). The Prozac Paradox W hy antidepressants m ay exacerbate depression and anxiety in some kids and teens. *Popular Science.* http://psychrights.org/articles/PopularScienceProzac Paradoxhtm

Mate, G., (1999). *Scattered: How Attention Deficit Disorder Originates And What You Can Do About It.* New York: The Penguin Group

McNuff, J., (2005). *Personal communications .* Paterson, NJ.

Medicating Kids: Interview with Russell Barkley. *PBS, Frontline.*
http://www.pbs.org/wgbh/pages/frontline/shows/medicating/interviews/ba
rkley.html

Mick, E. The relationship between stimulants and tic-disorders in
children treated for attention deficit hyperactivity disorder.
Harvard School of Public Health.
http://www.pubmedcentral.nih.gov/articlerender.fcgi?artid=2277289 and
http://www.hsph.harvard.edu

Mind Launches Green agenda for Mental Health. Ecotherapy vs.
retail therapy, (2007). *Heliq.com.* From Heliq database:
http://www.huliq.com/21526/mind-launches-new-green-agenda-for-
mental-health

Moody, S., (2007, April 15). Jefferson Award Presented to Dan Woldow--- San
Francisco Schools are kissing junk food goodbye. Here's Why. *San Francisco
Chronicle.* www.sfgate.com .

Moore, Daniel, T., Ph.D., (2001). Behavioral Interventions for ADHD.
http://www.yourfamilyclinic.com/shareware/addbehavior.html

Neven, R. Anderson, V. Godber, T., (1997). *Rethinking ADHD:
Integrated approaches to helping children at home and at school.*
Australia: Allen & Unwin.

New Jersey Teaching Notes, 2005-2009. New Jersey: AYCNP.

New Prozac Blues, (Dec 17, 2004). *Time Magazine.*
http://www.time.com/time/magazine/article/0,9171,1009635,00.html

Olfman, S., (2006). *No Child Left Different.* Praeger.

Olfman, S., (2007) . *Bipolar Children.* Praeger.

Pearce, J., (March 3, 2008). Peter Neaubauer, 94, Noted child
Psychiatrist. *New York Times.*
http://www.nytimes.com/2008/03/03/nyregion/03neubauer.html

Pharmacotherapy. *Center for Disease Control and Prevention.
Department of Health and Human Services.* http://www.cdc
.gov. (Retrieved December 2006).

Range, L. Children's Health. *Attention! For families and Adults with
Attention Deficit/Hyperactivity Disorder.* From: CHADD.

Rabiner, David., (2006). What is ADHD? *Attention Research Update.*
http://www.helpforadd.com /what-is-adhd

Ibid, (March, 2010). One Reason why Children with ADHD Should be Reevaluated
Each Year. *Attention Research Update newsletter.*

Ibid, (2006, January). Side effects rates for medications. *Attention Research Update.* Newsletter. http://www.helpforadd.com/2006/january.htm

Ratey, J. An Update on Medications used in the Treatment of Attention Deficit Disorder. *Attention Deficit Disorder Association (ADDA).* From ADDA database: www.add.org. Retrieved 2005.

Read for Emotional Relief, (2006). *Healthy Person.* www.healthy-person. blogspot.com/2006/11/read-for-emotional-relief.html

Remembering George Albee, (2006). *Society for Community Research and Action.* From website: www.scra27.org/George%20Albee.html

Richardson, W, (2005). ADHD and Stimulant Medication Abuse. *Attention Deficit Disorder Association (ADDA).* From ADHD database: www.add.org/articles/med_abuse.html

Rief, Sandra, F., (1993). *How to Reach and Teach ADD/ADHD Children.* Hoboken, NJ: Wiley & Sons.

Ritalin and Depression, (March 8, 2007). *Med TV.* http://adhd.emedtv.com/ritalin/ritalin-and-depression.htm

Robertson, J., (1998). *Natural Prozac.* San Francisco: HarperSanFrancisco.

Rupin, T. MD, Garrison, M. PhD, Christakis, MD, MPH, (November 5, 2006) A Systematic Review for the Effects of Television Viewing by Infants and Preschoolers. *Pediatrics.* pp.2025-2031.

Rxcom. (side effects list for medications). https://ecom.nhin.com/nhin/servlet/DrugSearchEntry?CHAIN_ID=119080

Ryals, Thad, F., MD. (Retrieved April 9, 2011) www.thadryals.com

Sachs, G. (March 28, 2007). Adding antidepressants to mood-stabilizing drugs does not affect (positively) bipolar depression (disorder.) study. *The New England Journal of Medicine*
.

Sigman, Dr. Aric, (2005). Remotely Controlled: How television is damaging our lives – and what we can do about it. London: Vermillion

Study Shows School Breakfast Program Works in Newark, (February 2010). *Essex News.* p.9

Schmidt, Barton, D., (1991). *Your Child's Health.* New York: Bantam.

Shannon, Scott M., M.D.; Heckman. E., (2007). *Please Don't Label My Child.* Rodale

Study finds early Ritalin exposure may have long term effects, (2004, December 20). *Mental Health Weekly.* Wiley Periodicals, Inc. www3.interscience.wiley.com

Szabo, L., (March 27, 2006). ADHD Treatment is Getting a Workout; Doctors Turn to Exercise, other Drug Alternatives. *USA Today*. www.usatoday.com

Focusing on Instruction. *Teach ADHD*. *http://research.aboutkidshealth.ca/teachadhd/teachingadhd/chapter6*

Timmes, A., (2005). ADHD Through the Eyes of Girls. *NJ County Family Magazine*. Moutainside, NJ.

Urie Bronfenbrenner, (2008). *New World Encyclopedia*. http://www.newworlde ncyclopedia.org/entry/Urie_Bronfenbrenner

Walker, Sydney III, (1998) *The Hyperactivity Hoax*. New York: St. Martin's Press.

Wallis, Claudia, (March 19, 2006). The Multitasking Generation. *Time Magazine*. www.time.com.

What is ADHD? Kids Health. (Retrieved August 14, 2009). http://kidshealth.org/parent/medical/learning/adhd.html

Wilens, T., (2006). Multisite controlled study of OROS methylphenidate in the treatment of adolescents with Attention-Deficit/Hyperactivity Disorder. *Archives of Pediatric and Adolescent Medicine*. 148(8), 859-861

Wilens, T. E., Faraone, S. V., Biederman, J., Gunawardene, S., (2003). Does Stimulant Therapy Of Attention-Deficit Hyperactivity Disorder Beget Later Substance Abuse A Meta-Analytic Review Of The Literature. *Pediatrics*, 111 179 185. *http://pediatrics.aappublications.org/cgi/content/abstract/111/1/179*

Williams, J. Zickler, P., (June 2003). Researchers Probe for Clues to ADHD Medications' Protective Effects. *National Institute on Drug Abuse*. http://archives.drugabuse.gov/NIDA_Notes/NNVol18N1/Researchers.html

Wolraich, M. L., M.D.; Wilson, D. B., Ph.D; White, W., M.D., (1995). The Effect of Sugar on Behavior or Cognition in Children. A Meta-analysis. *Jama* 274(20);1616-1621. http://jama.ama-assn.org/cgi/content/abstract/274/20/1617

Young, J; Giwerc, D. (2005). *Just What is Coaching? Attention Deficit Disorder Association (ADDA)*. From ADDA database: http://www.add.org.

Zimmerman, M., M.D.; Ruggero, C, Ph.D.; Chelminski, Ph.D., Young, D., Ph.D., (December 24, 2007). Is Bipolar Disorder Overdiagnosed? *The Journal of Clinical Psychiatry*. http://www.psychiatrist.com/abstracts/abstracts.asp?abstract=200806/060 808.htm

Index

Made in the USA
Lexington, KY
11 February 2012

13613579R00071